The Rest of God

The Rest of God

Finding Freedom from Lust in the Internet Age

Jay Haug

ISBN: 1532733585
ISBN 13: 9781532733581

"So if we are looking for what is most sacred in this world, all we need to do is look for that which is most often profaned. Is there any question at this moment of history what that is? The gift of the body and sexuality is under violent unrelenting attack."

THEOLOGY OF THE BODY EXPLAINED
BY CHRISTOPHER WEST

"Therefore let us be grateful for receiving a kingdom that cannot be shaken."

HEBREWS 12:28A

Dedication

This book is dedicated to the thousands of men and women living in lust recovery who remain sober, work their program every day, take phone calls from the desperate, and meet in cafes and church buildings with others who struggle as we do. They are living demonstrations of the "rest" of God spoken about in the Epistle to the Hebrews. They are walking miracles who shine brightly in a darkening world.

Index

Notes: Bible passages are taken from the ESV unless otherwise noted. In reference to God, Father Son and Holy Spirit, I do not capitalize the pronoun "his" or "him." No offense is intended. I would like to thank my dear wife Claudia for her editorial expertise.

Preface

This book is inspired by my own experience in lust and sex addiction recovery and the desire to see the 21st century church employ the fullest and most authentic ministry of the gospel possible to fallen humans. Now more than ever, church leaders must demonstrate gospel application to real and substantial human problems, lest we marginalize ourselves by wandering away into abstract theology. Instead, we must search for kingdom preaching rooted in the human condition and especially in the human heart.

I and many others owe a debt of gratitude to Ron J's reflections on his own similar recovery in his ground-breaking book Impossible Joy, which helped me to rediscover Jesus's ever-present availability to people like me, the weak, vulnerable and tempted. We in the lust recovery community are discovering that his presence makes all the difference in surrendering lust and temptation. Similarly, Pope John Paul II's Wednesday audience teachings organized as the Theology of the Body offer groundbreaking insights into the human condition, and real hope for "the redemption of our bodies." (Romans 8:23.) For easier understanding, quotations here are taken from Theology of the Body Explained by Christopher West.

We live in an age of forgetfulness, empowered by the immediacy of the internet. Similarly, the church has by and large forgotten how to apply the life-transforming message of the gospel to problems of addictive sexual behavior. In addition, all the research indicates that we in the church are in deep denial about Christian adults and children's involvement in internet porn. Now overwhelmed by these behaviors, we seem lost and listless to confront the burgeoning challenge of lust and sexually addictive behavior. In order to reach this generation, we must rediscover the immediate and accessible power of Jesus to overcome lust. Forsaking a futile individualistic approach, we have learned that the addicted person must live out their recovery in a 12 Step program in the context of transparent community if we are to remain "happy, joyous and free."

I make references to the 12 Steps throughout the book. The 12 Steps of Sexaholics Anonymous are listed at the end as an example of how lust recovery can be applied.

The writing that follows is not meant to be a commentary on the Epistle to the Hebrews. Rather, I attempt to demonstrate how relevant themes from it, as well as from the rest of the Bible, can be applied to practical human problems like sex addiction today. As we rediscover soul-care type teaching and preaching, we will find we have a ready audience eager to apply some of the principles outlined here, ones that promise not only increasing freedom in this life, but eternal bliss in "the city that is to come." (Hebrews 13:14)

Finally, "the rest of God" is an intentional double entendre. Not only has God made provision for our spiritual and ultimate rest from all sin and addiction in Jesus Christ, which is the message of Hebrews. But as an added bonus, those who find that rest may also discover aspects of God's character they never knew existed. Read on.

Jay Haug
Summer 2016

Introduction

WHY IT'S SO DIFFICULT FOR THE CHURCH TO TALK ABOUT SEX AND WHY WE MUST DO IT ANYWAY

I remember clearly my prep school English teacher reading Alexander Pope's famous lines from his Essay on Man.

> Know, then, thyself, presume not God to scan;
> The proper study of mankind is man.
> Placed on this isthmus of a middle state,
> A being darkly wise, and rudely great:
> With too much knowledge for the sceptic (sic) side,
> With too much weakness for the stoic's pride,
> He hangs between; in doubt to act, or rest;
> In doubt to deem himself a god, or beast;
> In doubt his mind or body to prefer;
> Born but to die, and reasoning but to err;
> Alike in ignorance, his reason such,
> Whether he thinks too little, or too much:
> Chaos of thought and passion, all confused;
> Still by himself abused, or disabused;
> Created half to rise, and half to fall;

Great lord of all things, yet a prey to all;
Sole judge of truth, in endless error hurled:
The glory, jest, and riddle of the world!

My teacher then quoted the middle lines.

"In doubt to deem himself a god, or beast
In doubt his mind or body to prefer;"

He then stated, "That is what Christianity is hung up on…sex."

When in my mid-twenties and preparing for ordained ministry, I dismissed my teacher's and other people's analyses of man's fall as being primarily about sex. As any junior theologian knows, the reasons for and effects of the fall are far more profound and consequential than sex alone.

And yet, as we look out on the landscape of both church and culture today, it seems that sex has indeed become our Achilles heal. Sex is at the heart of some of our deepest vulnerability and confusion. As I talk to Christian leaders about sexual addiction ministry in the context of the church, I hear one phrase over and over again, the "elephant in the room." Christian leaders tell me that pornography, illicit relationships, hook-ups and other sexually addictive behaviors are increasingly prevalent in their congregations. Just in the past months, I have spoken to several young clergy who have been forced to resign as the result of behaviors directly related to internet and technology use. They were considered "rising stars" by their peers before what was inside became public. I too resigned my position as an Episcopal clergyman in 1993 at the age of forty-two due to my acting out behavior.

I spoke to one pastor recently who described his congregation as "affluent on the outside, broken on the inside." Whether the appearance of the elephant is due to internet porn or the web's greasing the wheels for sexual hook ups, we are clearly facing a major challenge, one that is both inside and outside the church. Here is some chilling research on the subject.

- 80% of 500 Christian men surveyed at a men's retreat admitted they were feeling disconnected from God because lust, porn, or fantasy had gained a foothold in their lives (Pastors.com, reported by Kenny Luck from Saddleback Church)
- 70% of Christians admitted to struggling with porn in their daily lives (poll taken by XXX Church, as reported on CNN)
- 64% of Christian Pastors and leaders confirm that they are struggling with sexual addiction or sexual compulsion including, but not limited to use of pornography, compulsive masturbation, or other secret sexual activity ("Men's Secret Ways" Patric Means Confidential Survey)
- 51% of pastors say cyber porn is a temptation. 37% say it is a current struggle (Christianity Today, Leadership Survey, 12/2001)

All the evidence suggests that a large and uncontrollable shadow is being cast over the 21st century church as the secret sin stalks us with persistent steps. In my own preparation for ordained ministry years, my required psychological and vocational suitability report indicated the presence of a "'shadow," that the psychologist described as "occasional mild depression." But it turned out the shadow was in fact much more pervasive and threatening. Robert Lewis Stevenson may have been writing more profoundly than he knew, when he wrote the following poem called My Shadow.

I have a little shadow that goes in and out with me,
And what can be the use of him is more than I can see.
He is very, very like me from the heels up to the head;
And I see him jump before me, when I jump into my bed.

The funniest thing about him is the way he likes to grow—
Not at all like proper children, which is always very slow;

For he sometimes shoots up taller like an india-rubber ball,
And he sometimes gets so little that there's none of him at all.

He hasn't got a notion of how children ought to play,
And can only make a fool of me in every sort of way.
He stays so close beside me, he's a coward you can see;
I'd think shame to stick to nursie as that shadow sticks to me!

When we survey the cultural scene today, we can only conclude that the shadow of lust, the unruly child who comes and goes seemingly at will, is sticking to us and we are not quite sure how to handle him. Recognizing that every congregation is different in its culture and openness to dealing with these matters, we might well ask, "Why is it so difficult for the church to talk about sex and confront such a widespread problem?" Here are some reasons.

First, sex is powerful. Everyone knows this and it makes things difficult. Sex is akin to nuclear energy. Used in the manner for which it was created, for a constructive purpose, and with the right safe-guards, both nuclear power and sex are wonderful things. Years ago, I ran a road race by the Three Mile Island nuclear reactor. Part of the race was promotional: After several years of clean up, the owners wanted to show that the area was perfectly safe. But we all know the downside of nuclear energy. Unleashed outside the constraints of clean energy use, nuclear power can wreak untold havoc and destructive power. Much of the West is deeply suspicious today of Iran because it does not believe Iran will use nuclear technology for good. The force is only as good as the people using it. So it is with sex. Today, many are struggling with their own powerlessness in the face of illicit sex.

A great example of powerlessness in the face of sexual temptation is the Song "Say No to This" from the smash-hit Broadway musical *Hamilton*. Hamilton and Maria Reynolds recount in song the motivation, progression, and web of deception that led them into and out of their affair, one that cost them both dearly.

We see the power of sex today and our inability to control it in many ways, marital infidelity, the virtual daily reports of child sex abuse and child pornography arrests, and the general fueling of lust by visual stimuli. Does the gospel have any word to speak to this ubiquitous power? Writer Ron J in his book **Lust Virus** writes that men have been programmed through visual stimuli to be practitioners of "pseudo-sexuality," a kind of false sexuality that works against the self, intimacy with women, and any experience of sexual freedom. Despite these developments, the church today too often does not proactively teach about our sexuality, assumes the safeguards are in place among our congregants, and is shocked to find particular instances of lust's destructive power. We often have no answer to it except to pick up the pieces and send people off to counseling. Furthermore, because few Christians talk about this, many feel isolated because they believe they are the only ones struggling. We are missing a very large opportunity.

Secondly, sex is mysterious. The Apostle Paul speaks about the "mystery of the union between Christ and His Church." Of all the images brought to mind, Paul chooses a sexual one to speak of the union between Christ and his people. Marriage is sacred partly because it exists as a human icon pointing forward to "the marriage supper of the lamb," the eternal spousal union between Christ and the church. It took John Paul II nearly two hundred Wednesday audience lectures to unpack his Theology of the Body, which plumbs the depths of the Bible's teaching on sexuality and the body and what he calls the "Great Mystery." The mystery of Christ's union with us and the mystery of the sexual union between wife and husband are both…you guessed it, mysterious!

But biblical mysteries are not conundrums but rather "secrets revealed," realities that can indeed be spoken about. Most clergy realize that in speaking about sexuality at all, they are treading on holy ground. Too often, rather than entering this difficult territory, we demur, desiring to avoid speaking wrongly or inaccurately. In the presence of the holy, words fail us. Rather than write weak and pedestrian verse, the young lover lets Hallmark do it for him, lest he appear an inarticulate dunce in the presence of his beloved. So because it is hard to talk about sex, we don't.

The biblical writers differed. How many Christians would find it embarrassing to listen to the suggestive verses of Song of Songs with its overt description of body parts?

Your breasts are like two fawns,
    like twin fawns of a gazelle
    that browse among the lilies. (Song of Songs 4:5)

Moreover, the New Testament writers were not afraid to talk about lust. The Apostle Peter was unabashed when he encouraged his hearers to follow Christ, "having escaped the corruption that is in the world through lust." (2 Peter 1:4 KJV) If lust is such a powerful force in man's corruption, should we not be talking about it? Moreover, we are often ill-versed in the spiritual aspects of sexual love, so we simply refuse to engage with sexuality as a necessary biblical subject, let alone a pressing personal issue. Like a new and unfamiliar firework on the 4ᵗʰ of July, we leave it in the box, rather than blow ourselves up.

If sex is challenging to talk about, lust is even more difficult to broach. Perhaps this is due to shame attached to our sexuality because of our upbringings, past activities, or our current thought life. Lust, when it involves a married person, can be a threat to the marriage itself. Many enter marriage falsely believing it will cure lust. Many have learned through painful experience it does not.

Another roadblock to airing this problem is that clergy rightly believe they are supposed to support marriages rather than undermine them. Raising an issue like lust can seem counter-productive for the very marriages these leaders would like to see healed. Do pastors ignore the subject hoping things will turn around for their vulnerable members or provoke a crisis by raising the subject, hoping for a breakthrough? Furthermore, it is difficult for men to share their problem with lust because it often unearths a hidden conflict. Rather than wake the sleeping lust dog and create problems, we would rather let him lie. When indulging lust, men often tell themselves, "I can handle this," even though by feeding their false selves through internet porn and other addictive behaviors, the lust monster may be growing stronger and roaming farther and wider from home, accelerating the day of reckoning. Unless a person has surrendered lust, why would he or she bring it up, stoking anxiety in spouses and family? Make no mistake. There are reasons to avoid the whole subject.

Much of the talk of illicit sex in Christian communities focuses on changing certain behaviors or putting accountability in place to solve it. But accountability can only support prior surrender. It cannot create it. In our experience, lust is the core issue in sexual addiction, not the behaviors it leads to. As Jesus said in Matthew 5:27-28,

27 "You have heard that it was said, 'You shall not commit adultery.'[a] 28 But I tell you that anyone who looks at a woman lustfully has already committed adultery with her in his heart." Christianity is a religion of the heart. Changing outward behaviors is futile without engaging the well-spring from which they come. There are many illicit sexual behaviors that trouble human beings. What they all share is lust. If we can surrender lust, we are on the way to letting go of the behaviors it leads to.

And yet, lust remains too often today mired in lists uttered by preachers and teachers, rarely singled out as the "elephant in the room" it has actually become. I have been told by more than one gentleman that these are "private matters." Many of us do not want our private matters known publicly. In any case, there are plenty of ways to deal with this privately, they say. And they are correct. But do we?

The truth is a church member may not approach their pastor until they know he or she is sympathetic and at least somewhat knowledge-able about the problem. Many men who attend sexual addiction recovery groups have not yet told their pastor. Is this from fear of rejection? Or do they believe their pastor might not understand or accept their struggle? Do they believe the pastor will simply call them to repent, not appreci-ating that they have spent a thousand nights "repenting" only to return to their folly? This is why we believe it is vital for pastors, priests and church leaders to publicly state their awareness of the problem several times a year, encouraging people to talk with them about it. Our ministry, Jacob's Well (www.jacobswellhope.com) has resources to equip busy pas-tors to help men and women in their congregations.

Finally, in the minds of many Christian leaders, talking about lust is the "third rail" of ministry, akin to meddling or undermining their own careers. Why upset people, expose men and provoke fear in women when this is all so unnecessary? And we have not even broached the fact reported by Covenant Eyes (www.covenanteyes.com) that upwards of 30% of pornography consumers are now women. Better to stay away.

All this is taking place in a culture in which "sexuality" is now akin to what "soul" used to mean in people's minds. Sexuality has now become "who I am," an identity often divorced from the physical bodies God gave us and undergirded by shifting, self-definitions defended by political agendas. To many Christian leaders, mentioning sexuality can feel like wandering into a mine field. A recent young pastor in the Washington D.C. area remarked to me how many battles with people in his church involve conflicting understandings of sexuality.

Another problem is the issue of multi-generational audiences in a church context. Because we want to keep families together, we don't want to unnecessarily separate the generations and sexes. It is difficult to talk about sex because our teaching may be appropriate for some but not for others. Let's face it, we can make illusions to this on Sunday mornings, but with teens, children, parents and grandparents all in the pews together, (isn't this what we are after?) we just can't get too specific. And even when we separate the men and talk about it, fear arises when their wives ask the inevitable question after they come home, "What did you talk about?" The reply "It's confidential," simply raises more fear.

The above constitutes a grim scenario. But it does not need to be this way. In fact, I believe that those who grasp the nettle and are willing to speak clearly and compassionately about sex and lust will find mostly relief in their hearers. People already know what a problem all this is. Just ask your 18-35 year old friends or children.

Let me be clear. In calling upon the church to speak about sexuality, I am not advocating the kind of graphic, mechanical language that books about sex often employ. What we need is more teaching and witness concerning the spiritual, vocational and emotional aspects of sexuality and marriage and the purpose for which God made us. This is what people long to hear about and understand. We are learning it is not enough to stand against cultural trends.

So why must we talk about sex, at least in some congregational context today? Here are just a few reasons.

First, our sexuality is important to God. Our sexuality is part of our souls. It impinges directly on our minds, wills and emotions. God created it and designed its use. It makes sense that a discussion with the original manufacturer with the manual open might help. Too often, we have shied away from speaking of sexuality because we fear it. We would prefer to banish it to the worldly realm. The result is that the world has turned around and defined it back for us and our children. God's design is that we understand his purposes for us, including our sexuality.

Yes, sex is not everything. But many want to know how it becomes optional for them, instead of the compulsive, insistent, lust-driven force sex has become today. How do we thrive without engaging lust? Despite living in a sexualized culture, we may be forced to be celibate or choose to be so for long periods in our lives, due to singleness, separation, pregnancy, disease, an unwilling partner or by voluntary abstinence. How do we live in sexual freedom? These are important questions.

In our experience, for the sexually addicted and the single, sex must become optional to experience true sexual sobriety. Our "must have" relationship with sex gets us in trouble. Returning it to the optional category is one of the primary goals of recovery. But because sex is part of who we are as individuals and the outward and visible sign of the inward and spiritual union with our spouse, and is an expression of that intimacy, sex is important to us and therefore to God. Coming to terms with our sexuality is a significant part of our on-going discipleship.

Those of us who are Christians and share a long-term commitment to recovery believe that Jesus is the only one who has the answer to lust and sexual addiction. Why? Because fundamentally the lust-drive is a spiritual quest for connection, one that is designed to be fulfilled in him and helped along in community by others committed to sobriety and recovery. The "spiritual experience" essential to the early AA's was not optional. It was the basis for "letting go" of addictive behavior and giving oneself in service to others.

What about those who will not change or see nothing wrong with internet porn use and other lust driven behaviors? We cannot trouble ourselves over those who at least for the moment think there is nothing wrong with internet porn, masturbation and hook-ups. According to Covenant Eyes, this number among teens, including boys and girls is about 40% of the population. They may not be open to admitting their problem today. However, many will seek help when they experience the consequences of the path to which they have surrendered.

But there is a large group in the church looking for answers. If you would like a brief treatment of how to speak to them from a Christian perspective, pick up a copy of my book, Speaking to the Addictive Personality in the Local Congregation: A Guide for Pastors and Preachers. A larger treatment that will inspire anyone is Impossible Joy by Ron J. which deals specifically with lust recovery. More than any other book outside Scripture, Impossible Joy has given me an appreciation of Jesus' humanity and what it means for us, The truth is that the gospel in all its fullness and Jesus presence in the now of our temptation possess what the thirsty addictive soul is looking for, namely connection, a divine connection with the living God and transparent fellowship with those who struggle. This is why we strongly recommend lust addicts join a 12 Step fellowship of some kind or at least a group of people who struggle with lust.

A note of caution: Our experience has shown us that 12 Step groups welcoming "all addictions" do not work as our primary recovery fellowship for a number of reasons too numerous to mention here. We highly recommend those who struggle with lust join groups consisting of those who struggle as we do.

When we have the courage to speak about lust again, we will be speaking to the yearning of human hearts. For years, I have sat in churches wishing preachers would speak to what is really going on. Many do. But too often, the preacher is attempting to drag the congregation into the first century biblical world, as if by doing so, we will suddenly become enamored of that world and become the people God intended us to be. What should be happening is what did happen in that first century world, namely that Jesus entered it, spoke about the human heart in present day terminology and left us the legacy of transformation. He met individuals with specific problems. He spoke to them with compassion, touched their infirmities, and then carried their temptations, brokenness and idolatry to the cross and ended the separation from the Father. So today, Jesus wants to enter my world, the internet-driven, lust-filled world, overrun with "connection seekers" looking to fill their emptiness.

Either we speak to this world or we become irrelevant. Either there is a gospel for this world or we perish. If we can learn to speak about God's provision for sexual brokenness in a biblical, respectful, contextualized, helpful and compassionate way, we will begin to see lives changed right before us. The sermon must not be about what the passage says alone. If we speak about the current struggle and use Scripture to proclaim the good news about it, hearts will be transformed.

When we speak about lust again, we will find a new bridge to needy people. The old saw about the church "answering questions no one is asking" can sometimes ring true. Much of the world believes the church has no relevance today. Part of the reason is that the world sees into our "religious" souls more than we are willing to acknowledge. What does it see? It sees either "good" people to whom it cannot relate or people pretending to be something they are not. Both of these conclusions result in a lack of identification and "turning off" to the church.

The odd reality is this: we in the church are being forced into speaking about lust and sex. The plague of sexual addiction, among our own people and outsiders, is right in our faces. A few days ago, I ran into a old sex addiction recovery friend in the supermarket. He asked what I was doing these days and I happily gave him my Jacob's Well business card. He said he had a friend who was struggling who might be interested in finding help. Before I could respond he said, "It's everywhere."

Now more than ever, we cannot turn away or retreat into our holy huddle with a pharisaic sigh of relief that we are not like these lust-driven people out in the world. The truth is that we are one with them in vulnerability, even when lust is not our core issue, and it is that very vulnerability which can build bridges to them. This is what Paul meant when he said, "To the weak, I became weak to win the weak." (1 Corinthians 9:22). There is a reason that in recovery groups, we lead with weakness.

When the Christian gospel broke upon the world, believers spoke a bold and compassionate message to a sex drenched, pagan world. We have the message if we will but learn to speak it again, the way Augustine did in his **Confessions,** the way the Apostle Paul did when he spoke of his thorn in his flesh in 2 Corinthians 12, in our calling to comfort those the way we ourselves have been comforted in 2 Corinthians 1, and in the way Christians in recovery from sexual addiction are doing so today.

For all these reasons and more, we must speak about sex once again. If we believe the gospel, in a Redeemer who experienced every temptation known to man, (Hebrews 4:15), and in His living presence in our midst, who is the living water to a thirsty world, we will rediscover in our day how to do as the angel commanded the Apostle Peter in Acts 5:20. "Go, stand and speak in the temple to the people all the words of this life."

Some final thoughts. I recognize that there are many ancillary issues raised by the topic of lust and sexual addiction. Human trafficking, pornography laws, sexual abuse of adults and children all are worthy topics. However, we will not deal with any of them in this volume, except in passing. Our focus here is on the core issue that drives them all. Were the entire world suddenly be empowered to surrender lust, none of these problems would exist. Neither will we consider the wounds, problems and recovery of the spouses and family members of those habitually engaging in lust, an entire subject worthy of discussion and compassionate ministry. By staying focused on what Jesus defined as the core issue, we hope to more fully understand the gospel provision for its relief. I will share some highly detailed personal history in this book, experiences echoed in thousands of other lives. I do so for the sole purpose of demonstrating the power of Jesus to overcome personal struggles. If even one person reads this believing they are "too far gone" to surrender lust and as a result finds hope and help, I will be happy beyond words.

One

*It helped me a great deal to become convinced that
alcoholism was a disease, not a moral issue; that I
had been drinking as a result of a compulsion...*

Alcoholics Anonymous, p. 416.

*(Referring to Adam and Eve) Once they gave into that
temptation, their freedom was invaded by attachment.
They experienced the need for more. God knew that they
would not—could not—stop with just the one tree."*

Gerald May, Addiction and Grace

Before we venture into the text of Hebrews itself, we must understand the idea of lust and why it is the foundational issue for those dealing with sex addiction in any form. Before any discussion of remedies as they relate to behaviors, boundaries, accountability and all the other issues surrounding recovery, we must come to terms with the driving force at work. If we fail to do this, we will simply be papering over the cracks of addiction or imposing law from the outside, which we know does not work. We would not be addressing the real problem.

It is absolutely essential that Christian leaders understand that the foundations of lust are spiritual in nature. If we miss this, we will be unable to properly minister to people who struggle with pornography and sexual sin of all kinds.

The human being who has surrendered to sexual addiction has "taken himself or herself out of the whole context of what is right or wrong." (Sexaholics Anonymous, page 202) This is an important truth. What it means, among many things, is that appeals to morality as the root cause or possible solution to acting out sexually have no power to heal in cases of long-term sexual addiction. The lust addict has normally used numerous moral upbraidings on himself or herself for years. He or she has no doubt spent many a morning both recounting and regretting the night before, or prior behavior in general. We lust addicts are people who know exactly what the right thing to do is but find ourselves without the resources in ourselves to do it. This utter powerlessness initially produces remorse, pain and many a resolution. What it does not produce is change.

Part of the pain we experience is due to a God-given spiritual violation we can sense internally. This occurs when we fail to see another person properly as someone in the totality of their personhood, with a will and a body that only they can give. Instead, lust occurs when we attempt to take it, either visually or actually, often over-riding another's deliberate choice, taking something rather than giving it. We damage what Pope John Paul II calls the "inner inviolability of the person." When we do this, "We take what is not given. We become master over another person. And persons— precisely because they are persons—are meant to be their own masters. Their dignity demands it." In his words we are attempting to engage in "the impossibility, as it were, of one person being appropriated and mastered by the other." (Theology of the Body Explained, p. 486)

The Church often refers to pastors and other people suffering the consequences of their behavior as those who have experienced a "moral failure," but what has actually happened is a "spiritual failure." This is why early 12 Steppers spoke of an "authentic spiritual experience" as necessary for recovery prior to any moral change. Renewed morality follows renewed spirituality. It is powerless to lead it. Even a cursory reading of the Epistle to the Romans leaves us with exactly this message.

Therefore, there is now no condemnation for those who are in Christ Jesus, [2] because through Christ Jesus the law of the Spirit who gives life has set you[a] free from the law of sin and death. (Romans 8:1)

The "Spirit who gives life" produces change, not the moral will of human effort, not this "law of sin and death" which traps us endlessly in the cycle of addiction. John 1:12 speaks of a similar new birth apart from morality or human will. [12] But to all who did receive him, who believed in his name, he gave the right to become children of God,[13] who were born, not of blood nor of the will of the flesh nor of the will of man, but of God.

A Spiritual Misconnection

The essence of sexual addiction is a misconnection or a false spiritual connection. This is why the Bible spends so much time talking about idolatry, which is the essence of this false spiritual connection, the attempt to derive God-like results from things that claim to deliver us but ultimately cannot. Because humans derive their identity from God, we are the only creatures who possess a spirit, one that is filled with the unique breath of God himself.

Then the LORD God formed a man from the dust of the ground and breathed into his nostrils the breath of life, and the man became a living being. (Genesis 2:7)

We are therefore given the opportunity of making spiritual connections in many forms and in many arenas. When we surrender our spirit to someone or something, we receive the spirit of whatever we engage with in return. This is why idolatry is so dangerous, because it transmits attitudes and values that comingle with our spirits. Alcoholism, materialism, lust, resentment in combative relationships, and so many other things all infuse the one who indulges in them with the spirit that animates this particular relationship. Unfortunately, the lust addict or sexaholic has established a pattern, usually over years or decades, of reaching out for the false connection and engaging with picture lust or bodies pre-programmed by the addictive brain as sex objects. Research concerning neural pathways in the brain has confirmed the reality of this recurring lust connection syndrome which constantly draws us back.

Many Christians I know are currently trapped in a cycle of despair that stems from behavior that defines their private life. Pornography, masturbation, internet relationships all make up a life that confounds them. How can this be happening when they are believers, are regularly practicing their faith and are possessed of Biblical knowledge? One of my recovering friends testifies that his point of deepest addiction was precisely at the zenith of his ecclesiastical career. There could be many reasons for these phenomena, but one reality defines them all. "Religion" cannot save us when our spirits are idolatrous. Religion and idolatry can exist in the same person at the same time! I know because I lived it. This is not new.

Jesus saw this in his time and quoted Isaiah in response to it. "'These people honor me with their lips, but their hearts are far from me." (Matthew 15:8) What we do in our most private moments, unrestrained by human eyes, is who we really are. Many therapists must work diligently with clients to combat the dissociative drive which keeps this deep denial in place. As many will testify, in such secret, private moments morality is virtually powerless to stop what they have come to believe is their inevitable path to act out.

Humans are designed by God to make spiritual connections with others, either healthy spiritual connections or damaging ones. Have you ever wondered why the Apostle Paul says, "Do you not know that he who unites himself with a prostitute is one with her in body? For it is said, "The two will become one flesh." (1 Corinthians 6:16) Paul cannot mean, "Do you not know that he who unites himself with a prostitute has sex with her." No, everyone admits that he means something deeper, brought about by sexual intercourse. He is saying, "There is a lasting connection here, even if it involves a financial transaction." Consequences follow actions.

Looking back on my own life, I thought for years that illicit sex was my attempt to escape depression, the "shadow." I now believe that illicit sex was the depression's cause. These violations that occur against our spirits, our purpose and values, our very selves are damaging no matter how we try to justify, normalize or explain them away. This is how influential connections, both false and true ones, are to human beings. We all make them. The only question is what kind of connections we will make.

A number of years ago, a young women went to her college psychological clinic because she was depressed. The psychologist talked to her for several weeks about her upbringing, her relationship with her parents and siblings, current stresses, sleep patterns, alcohol use and so on. But try as he might the psychologist was unable to diagnose the depression's cause and the young woman felt no better. But if the therapist had been more thorough, he might have unearthed the fact that this young woman had engaged in sexual intercourse with two different men in the last month. It turned out that this sexual behavior, which went against her values and troubled her deeply was the actual source of the depression. The guilt, shame, remorse and confusion she felt was making her depressed. But because promiscuity is often dismissed as a root problem in certain cultural circles, its resulting consequences are also often missed. What happens between two people, particularly in the spiritual connection of sexuality can have an enormous impact on their lives.

What is wrong with us? The prophet Jeremiah knew.

"My people have committed two sins:
They have forsaken me,
      the spring of living water,
and have dug their own cisterns,
      broken cisterns that cannot hold water. (Jeremiah 2:13)

When a Christian engages in lust, what actually happens is that we turn away from God and forsake him in the moment. We then dig our own pornography cistern, the leaky vessel of lust and become secretive and dishonest in our relationship with others. More than half of married men who struggle with porn say that no one knows about their struggle. A

Christian who lusts has three aspects of detachment going on. He or she is detaching from God, detaching from other people and detaching from their true selves. This is the cistern of lust. Its costs are alienation, dishonesty and idolatry.

In a recent Time Magazine article entitled "Porn and the Threat to Virility," a new movement to give up porn was discussed at length. The reason? Younger men are discovering that viewing porn threatens sexual potency and undermines physical and relational intimacy. Alexander Rhodes said, "I thought it was normal to fantasize about porn while having sex with another person...He quit porn several times before finally swearing it off for good in 2013." We are discovering that porn actually undermines the beauty and connection of authentic sexuality. "Quitting porn is one of the most sex-positive things people can do," says Rhodes. Though the secular world does not see porn in overt spiritual terms, the physical, relational and psychological effects of both using it and surrendering it are real and lasting.

The reason lust is a spiritual disease is that like all addictions, it is instigated and agitated by underlying spiritual issues. Like all substances, initial use may simply be for pleasure, but continued compulsive use is driven by character defects of resentment, control, self-centeredness, ego and fear. The substance takes on god-like qualities as we medicate ourselves repeatedly, in this case with god of lust. This is the false spiritual connection that has run us ragged and ruined our lives, resulting in the long-term reality of broken relationships with God and others.

The irony of lust-addicts looking for connection is that we inevitably become isolated people. We become "people apart" alternately believing ourselves to be "special," either superior in our entitlement or inferior in our shameful behavior. We cannot understand and accept that we are simply human, wanting to connect and in desperate need of fellowship. The broken cistern of lust is readily available if only for the moment. The availability and free nature of internet porn make it easy to access unless a reason exists to turn away.

We must understand the proper relationship between cause and effect in sexual addiction. Years ago doctors would speak about how elderly people would "fall and break their hip." They portrayed the cause and effect this way, until recent times when they discovered that some elderly people actually break their hip first and then fall. This new understanding brought a different perspective toward the problem and the solution. Combating loss of bone density and strengthening the hip and surrounding area became as important as eliminating falls. So it is with sexual addiction. We must understand cause and effect here as well. The cause is spiritual, the effect moral. Until the spiritual is healed and redirected, there can be no moral change.

Let me be clear. I am not saying that the immoral behavior of the addict is of no significance. We know that the effects of it in terms of marriage, family life, vocation, mental and financial health can be devastating. But appeals to morality simply cannot instigate real change. The Apostle Paul makes a similar argument in Romans about the law's inability to save us;

[20] "Therefore no one will be declared righteous in God's sight by the works of the law; rather, through the law we become conscious of our sin. (Romans 3:20)

But the law still has value. "So then, the law is holy, and the commandment is holy, righteous and good." (Romans 7:12) The law is of value, just not "saving value." It cannot change a sex addict. I have known good theology and believed it for years. But having an excellent compass that points true north is only of value if you possess the power to travel to your desired destination. "Believing" without spiritual change is the essence of futility. Is this the reason there are about the same number of lust addicts in the church as outside it? We in the addiction-recovery community have learned through painful experience that appeals to morality will not work with most sex addicts, because neither our fall nor our recovery is about trying to be good.

A person struggling to stay sober will sometimes say. "I acted out yesterday but the good thing is that I am not beating myself up about it." A person who says this is attempting to offset a bad moral outcome with a good one, somehow believing that grading on a curve is the desired goal. How much better to simply admit our failings without reservation and recommit ourselves to our program without the false buffer of our own imagined goodness. In fact, attempts to be good are often indications of our deep-seated powerlessness. We have all failed at the attempt. Didn't Jesus say we would when he said, "No one is good but God alone?" (Mark 10:18) Didn't Paul assert this when he said, quoting Psalm 14, "As it is written, No one is righteous, not even one?" (Romans 3:10). Too many Christians read these words and think they apply to non-Christians. But they apply to all humanity.

Most of us have condemned our own immoral behavior for years, to no effect and even wept tears that felt like repentance at the time. We are people who have experienced deep shame. Morality with its unbending laws, humanly elevated winners (good people) and losers (bad people) and church-driven public exposure too often work against real recovery. (Note: I am not saying that church discipline should not be exercised. It should, but always to serve the intended purpose of spiritual restoration.)

What the Christian addict needs is an authentic connection with God and his Son Jesus Christ, one that appropriates something of his radical identification with our fallen humanity and his availability to bear our lust away in the very moment it occurs. We also need connection with those who struggle as we do and with compassionate, transparent, relatively healthy others as well. We must have the authentically human and divine connection we are looking for or we die spiritually. It is this connection that saves us, not appeals to morality or a false and often fleeting "repentance" that seeks to be the cause rather than the result of spiritual change. The spiritual gives birth to the moral, not the reverse.

Years ago the Oxford Group, which came to be known as "Moral Rearmament" helped to give birth to Alcoholics Anonymous. But a day of reckoning soon arrived. AA was growing as it reached out to the broken and helpless. At some point, The Oxford Group made a decision that they preferred not to be associated with "all these drunks." As a result, the Oxford Group passed into history. AA, with its emphasis on a "spiritual experience" offered to broken people is still growing. This message of the primacy of spiritual experience is the message of the New Testament. We should not be surprised to learn it is also the message of a recovery that works. There is so much more to learn and say about this topic. But all recovery ministry must begin here or it never begins.

But lets get practical and examine what this spiritual struggle looks like. A year or so ago, I wrote the following piece called "Lust: Before the Crash." It paints a spiritual portrait of an average Christian man struggling with lust before irreversible consequences set in.

He is a young professional, thirty-five or so, walking down the street of a major American city. The day is new, but his thoughts are not. He notices the women as they pass, the short skirts, the hints of cleavage, the eye contact they make with him or wishes they would make. He misses no attractive woman. Even when he pretends not to, the radar is always turned on. If you asked him, he would say this is the most ordinary of days. For him, all of this seems perfectly routine. And if this were the only thing he did, we might call him just an average man. But he is not an average man, because his outward behavior today and most days is spiritually connected to deeper inner wrongs that threaten to undo the nice suburban life he has managed to put together. Whether he knows it or not, he is living on the edge.

Our friend has learned to live with lust on call. In his honest moments, he admits it has been this way as long as he can remember. When in denial, he justifies himself that he is "just like other men." But last night, he looked at porn on his home computer. The wife he believes he loves was asleep in the next room. He even tucked in and prayed with his two young children, four and six. The adrenaline jolt he felt at the end of their prayer time caught his attention. Just a glimpse online, he told himself, but 90 minutes later, after losing track of time, he pulled himself away and finally logged off.

He knows he shouldn't do it, but somehow he can't stop. Do other guys have this problem? Certainly the guys at church don't, do they? It never occurs to him to call someone.

Things at work have not been going well in the last month, he muses as he walks. His boss is more demanding than ever. Moreover, the boss's stressed-out personality somehow radiates down the hall to our man's desk and envelopes his spirit multiple times a day. Sometimes, he wants to quit and do something else. But how can he walk away from the salary? What else would he do? He resents the boss, but don't most people? This low-grade yet noticeable resentment provides negative energy as he walks down the street. It agitates his soul. He rehearses comebacks he would like to say to his boss. "Bastard," he thinks. He wonders if there is any connection between the boiling resentment he feels and the relief-producing, temporary visual images that counteract his negative feelings.

Our subject is, believe it or not, a self-professed Christian. Yet at this moment, following on from last night, he is detached from the God he claims to believe in and trust. He has emotionally and spiritually checked out, turned his back on the Risen Jesus, the one who walks right beside him and longs to commune with him, the one he has confessed to being "alive" many times, the one who wants to bear his burdens away and take his temptations. But instead, the light adrenaline rush of seeing woman after woman lifts him to what he thinks is a better place. He turns his back, enters his private world, and detaches from who he really is. Without fully realizing it, he is living against his true self, setting up conflict in his deepest soul. This is the daylight version of nighttime porn. But the lust behind it is the same, a reality he has come to habitually dismiss. The pattern has been reinforced again and again. Having turned away, he finds himself alone with his lust, experientially separated from God. No matter what his theological beliefs, he is living out spiritual and relational separation. To make matters worse, he has reinforced this turning away by routine daily choices, isolating himself from other men who could share his burden in the moment it unfolds. It never occurs to him to call someone.

The truth is this is not just one, isolated, bright sunny day, much as he would like to see it that way. No, our subject is walking more of a well-worn path than he is willing to admit. In fact, since he discovered masturbation and pornography at the age of twelve, he has been routinely stoking the fires of lust in his heart. He thinks he is just a "normal red-blooded American." But he is not. He is caught in a trap he cannot escape. He is a prisoner of lust, a force he cannot control or limit by willpower. He tells himself he will never cheat on his wife. But his behavior makes it more likely that he will.. He is an accident waiting for an intersection.

He is:

"A young man without sense, passing along the street..." (Proverbs 7: 7b-8a NRSV)

"Right away he follows her
And goes like an ox to the slaughter,
Or bounds like a stag toward the trap
Until an arrow pierces its entrails.
He is like a bird rushing into a snare,
Not knowing it will cost him his life." (Proverbs 7:22-23 NRSV)

Something "spiritual" happened to him many years ago that is still in place. He became a man "apart" in his spirit. This began the day masturbation and rebellion joined forces in his young developing soul. Turning against his parents, authority figures and if truth be known, God himself, he found early the momentary but repetitive comfort of fantasy and masturbation. Sometimes the fantasy was inside, someone he saw, a remembered magazine image or a woman on television. Sometimes it was women's lingerie catalogs or porn. Whatever triggered lust was good enough. But something more was happening. A ritual was being born. When stress, fear, anger, isolation or loneliness fell upon him like a heavy blanket, the "friend" he turned to was lust and acting out. The feelings reinforced the behavior and vice-versa. The loop of negativity captured his soul.

For a time he thought marriage would save him, until he finally realized that his wife was far more than a ready-made outlet for his addiction. He loved her, but the fights and tension indicated something was wrong. He withdrew from her emotionally on a regular basis. What could he do? How could he change? Could he find another way to live? Why did he tense up when she entered the room? Why was she so disappointed with their marriage? What will happen to me? There were more questions than answers. But the rut remained in place.

How should we view our man? How can we help him? If anything in life is a "spiritual problem," this is. What might a spiritual solution look like? The "man apart," split off from reality, community and God himself must find a way to turn back to his true self and away from the "isolating obsession with sex and self." (The Solution, Sexaholics Anonymous, p. 202). He must find a way to honesty, enter a community of men who struggle as he does and get help. He must find the power of the admonition in James to "... confess your sins to one another and pray for one another that you may be healed." (James 5:16) He must find a healthy way to resolve character defects like resentment and self-centeredness and let go of the false solution of lust and acting out. He is likely to need to work the 12 Steps to live the life he wants to live, rather than the life he has been living. His future depends on it.

Tragically, too often a crash must come before recovery. The painful truth is that too many of us have had to experience the next stage, the painful one that awaits our man in the street. This next step will be extremely costly. He will engage sexually with a woman not his wife. It will 'cost him his life,' at least the life he has always known. His wife will discover the truth, sometimes sooner, sometimes much later. The marriage may survive and it may not. Perhaps then, the pain which he has so persistently avoided will cause him to admit his problem and he will begin to let go. Those who love him, if they know about his problem, hope that adultery will not have to happen. But one thing we do know. For the true sex addict, lust can only be surrendered. It cannot be "controlled." This we know: No amount of moralizing, self-remonstrating or regret will save him.

Fortunately, there is another way to live, a way of freedom, peace, and a newfound healthy connection with God and others. But it is a road designed to be travelled with others, not alone. It is paved with honesty. Its rewards are profound. If our man sounds anything like you, there is help, probably very near where you live.

Two

Sex Addiction and the Message of Hebrews

Sometimes I wake, and lo, I have forgot,
And drifted out upon an ebbing sea!
My soul that was at rest now resteth not,
For I am with myself and not with thee;
Truth seems a blind moon and a glaring morn,
Where nothing is but sick-heart vanity.

George MacDonald, Diary of an Old Soul

"Christians are usually sincere and well-intentioned
people until you get to the real issues of ego, control,
power, money, pleasure and security."

Richard Rohr

The whole idea of rest is the key to understanding the Epistle to the Hebrews. Its message is driven forward by this leitmotif, reaching its denouement in the final resting place for the people of God, "the city whose builder and maker is God." (Hebrews 11: 10 NIV) We live in an enormously restless culture. Sometimes this restlessness produces innovation, adventure and discovery. Without it, our world would stagnate. But the dark side of restlessness is that it can also eventuate in addictive behavior and a continuous search for the next high. So it is with sex addiction and the culture of "next" that has become almost like breathing for today's internet-based world, one where there is virtually no end to lust-based images and intrigue.

For the lust addicted person mired in restlessness, the next relationship, the next porn image, the next illicit act often presents itself as the "must have" thing. The internet provides a seemingly endless array of "next" because of its vast content available for the clicking. The internet is the mirror image of our restless selves, the supply closet for the searching soul. One very wise person expressed it this way. "Conning ourselves time and again that the next one would save us, we were really losing our lives. (Sexaholics Anonymous, p 203).

It is remarkable how our modern world misunderstands lust. During John Paul II's papacy, he addressed the issue of lust in marriage. Christopher West reports one reaction to it as follows. 'The Washington Post article that reported on (it) shows how much the secular media missed the "good news" of John Paul's call to sexual redemption. Judy Mann, in her article, "A Lesson on Lust for the Vatican," grants that the Pope's remarks were "motivated only by the best of intentions." However, she then goes on to inform the Pope that "he may not be familiar with the role lust plays in the American family…From the time Americans reach adolescence, lust is a life force." She concludes, "the Pope might want to bear in mind" that if "a man has lust in his heart for his wife, chances are he won't have adultery on his mind for someone else.".… These are the sad conclusions of the psychological interpretation of lust. Not only does it normalize lust. It asserts it as a good." (Theology of the Body Explained, p. 227.) Mann's defense of lust in marriage is false both psychologically and spiritually. The rooms of sexual addiction recovery are filled with people married to attractive spouses. None of these attractive spouses could save us. Mann's article fails to understand that lust cannot be controlled and enjoyed. It cannot be satiated, only surrendered.

A man who believes an attractive woman will cure him of lust is similar to the alcoholic who believes the most expensive bottle of bourbon, when consumed, will cure him of his desire to drink. It doesn't work that way. The only thing that does work is dealing with the problem with us, the desire to drink or lust. Therefore, asking any other person to fix our lust problem is doomed to failure.

So, how do we find rest in a sea of restlessness? How do find what Archimedes called "a place to stand," one that offers peace and perspective? Many of us who believe in Christ have found that intellectual assent is not enough. We have found that "right thinking" is insufficient to keep us sober and remove from us the problems of addictive behavior. There must be a deeper spiritual well from which to draw. I believe the Book of Hebrews sets forth this deeper spiritual message we are looking for. It is the gospel articulated in a context that is truly life-changing.

I have found in reading the Epistle to the Hebrews a counter-message to the acquisitive drive of lust, an anti-dote for a restless culture desperately searching for the next high. That great theme is finding "rest," something we sex addicts must indeed find if we are going to let go of our addiction. But how do we find it? Perhaps the first thing we must understand is that human nature has changed very little, which prompts the question: How are we lust and sex addicts like the Hebrew Christians of old? There are a number of parallels.

First, like these Jewish believers, Christian sex addicts often feel like displaced people. These first century Jewish believers had seen much in their day. They had witnessed the destruction of the temple (AD 66-70), the sacrificial system, and the priesthood. The very things put in place by God himself following the exodus, before the children of Israel entered the promised land, had now become obsolete. How could this be and how could they live in such a world?

How difficult it must have been to accept this change. Once Israel had ceased to wander in the wilderness, the only life they knew was as the people of a place, namely Jerusalem. Temple, priesthood and sacrifice became their routine. Those who lived in the surrounding country made their trip into the holy city at least three times a year, for Passover, Pentecost and Tabernacles. But now, since the fall of Jerusalem and the destruction of the temple, Jewish believers in Jesus were doubly disrupted. Not only had the temple been destroyed along with priesthood and sacrifice. Many of them had been also excommunicated from the synagogue once they confessed Jesus as the Messiah. (John 16:2) They clearly began to wonder where they fit in and felt themselves in danger of "shrinking back" to the old ways of law, ritual and sacrifice.

Many commentators believe the theme of the epistle is contained in Hebrews 10:39. "But we do not belong to those who shrink back and are destroyed, but to those who have faith and are saved." Jewish believers were discovering that their great temptation was to return to the old ways, to attempt to reconstitute that way of life with its familiar rituals, one they had struggled to achieve as a people, rather than move forward with faith in Jesus to find rest and an eternal city "not made with hands." The writer challenges them on precisely this point. "For here we do not have an enduring city, but we are looking for the city that is to come." (Hebrews 10:39). A people who had elevated a visible holy city in their minds, one which was now destroyed, would now be challenged to look beyond this physical world for their identity.

The stark reality for these Hebrew Christians was that they were no longer a people of a "place." In the universalizing of the gospel, they had become a people for all places and all times.

Addicts are often similarly displaced. When I confessed the true nature and extent of my addiction, I was instantaneously launched into a new and unfamiliar life with all its painful adjustments. In addition to receiving treatment for my addiction, I was now separated from my wife, living alone and seeking a new career. The disruption was so psychologically displacing that I experienced two panic attacks for the first and only time in my life and within a few months my body physically shut down, virtually the only part of me that had not "thrown in the towel" during my difficult adjustment. I became ill and missed four months of work. Just as I began my new career in the financial services industry, I had to start over yet again. Faith was not an abstract luxury for me. It was a moment by moment necessity.

The difference between the addict and the first century Jewish believer is stark in the following sense. The addict finds himself or herself displaced because of their own behavior, while the believer was simply the victim of circumstances beyond their control. Otherwise, they are exactly the same. Their former lives have suddenly evaporated, never to return. They must cope in a new world with new beliefs and understandings and a new approach to living. When helping repair marriages damaged by sexual addiction, we often tell people that there is no going back to the marriage as it was before. The only possible solution is a marriage based on news ways of acting, living and communicating. The Book of Hebrews lays that life out for both sets of people. This book will attempt to flesh out what some major aspects of that life is meant to be, with all of its challenges and possibilities. My purpose is to give hope to those who have ever asked themselves with the psalmist "Will the Lord reject forever? Will he never show his favor again? (Psalm 77:7) I say to you from my own experience, "hold on." Your life is about to become better than you have ever imagined. But you must let it unfold in God's time.

First century Jewish believers had to learn to live as a people of the Diaspora. In fact, Jews scattered throughout the world for centuries had never known anything else. But many others were driven out of Jerusalem into Asia Minor and beyond as a result of both Jewish and Roman persecution. Some, in the early days of the Way, stayed in Jerusalem and became part of a church that was so poor that the Apostle Paul spent much of his missionary efforts collecting an offering against its impending starvation. (2 Corinthians 8)

Many of these Jewish believers lived to see the Gentile mission become pre-eminent in the spread of the gospel, displacing the Jewish numerical superiority of the early Jerusalem Church. Though both Jesus (Matthew 15:24) and Paul (Romans 1:16) had expressed a call that began first with a mission to Jews, within the first 25 years after Jesus' death and resurrection, the Christian movement was fueled primarily by gentile conversions. Many Jewish believers heard stories of Paul's persecution by the Jews in the synagogues of Asia Minor. (Acts 14:1) As the Gentile mission flourished, they must have wondered what God's plan had become for them as a people. Paul wrestled with this question himself and wrote Romans 9-11 to specifically address the anxieties of Jewish believers, fearful that God may have written them off. Paul assured them that God had not forgotten them and that the inclusion of the Gentiles will simply precede and not supplant an ultimate Jewish turning to Jesus. (Romans 11:11-12) These Hebrew Christians had lost much. They were torn from a familiar and proud past and hurled into an uncertain future. Many became graphically displaced. They all had to learn to live in a different world, one that would both continually challenge and help to grow their faith.

If you are a Christian addict, particularly someone who has struggled with lust, pornography and sexual addition, there is good news for you. God still wants you. Jesus still loves you. If you don't believe this, please read the Book of Hosea. He desires to make your "Valley of Achor (which means Valley of Trouble) a door of hope." (Hosea 2:15) God wants to use you, perhaps now more than ever, in the lives of those who struggle as you do. The crashing down of a personality edifice built over many years is no more an impediment to God than the destruction of the Temple. In fact, it can lead to a greater mission field than you could ever know, just as it did for them.

Like these Hebrew Christians, when we accept that the past is over and we begin to address our fears and doubts about the future, perhaps for the first time, the pain can seem almost too much. Not only do we have to make life adjustments, job or career shifts, or marital and living changes, but we also have to deal with our stuff, our pain. Sometimes we think it will never end. But it does if we move through it one day at a time and find the grace to surrender. We suddenly discover there is much for us to do on the other side.

I remember in the midst of very early days in recovery, when I was experiencing intense pain, a therapist asked me to dive into more pain. It had to be done but I sure did not want to do it. One of the deep dives into pain can involve disclosure to our spouse or family. This can actually exacerbate further pain which can continue for a while. Once the dam of denial is burst, the floodwaters keep on coming for days on end bearing their wounding power. But the pain does eventually subside. The flood waters are replaced by healing waters. Finally, the consequences begin to ebb. Slowly, we get our life back, though in a different form. This process often stays in our memory banks as a living reminder of the power of choice and a reminder that if "we go back out there," the entire process can repeat itself.

Paul Simon in his song "The Boxer" contemplates the man struck down in life.

> In the clearing stands a boxer,
> And a fighter by his trade
> And he carries the reminders
> Of ev'ry glove that laid him down
> And cut him till he cried out
> In his anger and his shame,
> "I am leaving, I am leaving."
> But the fighter still remains.

Despite our being cut down by addiction, the fighter in us remains with both a story to tell for others and battle to fight for people just like us. We discover that the good news is even greater than we thought and that we are more resilient because of Jesus than we ever thought we could be.

Have you ever asked yourself, what is the worst event in the history of the world? Was it The Fall? The Holocaust? The Black Plague? All these events affected millions. But from a Christian perspective, the answer must be The Cross. God came to man and took on flesh and we killed him. Neitzsche wrote in his Parable of the Madman, "Where has God gone? He cried, "I shall tell you. We have killed him-you and I. We are his murderers." Neitzsche was referring to more of a philosophical movement than an historic deed, but the truth of that historic deed is echoed here. Jesus came and humanity put him to death.

But lets turn the question around. "What is the best event in the history of the world? Again, we might respond with numerous possibilities. The defeat of smallpox or polio? The Renaissance? The fall of the Soviet Union or Ottoman Empires? Hitler's demise? But from a Christian perspective, the answer is the same! The Cross. We call the day we celebrate it Good Friday. Of course we could certainly argue the Resurrection as the best event. But the power of the Resurrection is derivative. There can be no resurrection without the Cross, what John's gospel refers to as Jesus's "glorification." (John 17:5)

But what does this mean for us, practically speaking? It means that the seeds of victory, spiritual growth and freedom are bound up in our greatest weaknesses, faults and character defects. Part of the reason the devil wanted to get rid of Jesus was motivated by the mistaken belief that he could eliminate in man's mind the possibility that God could ever reverse the curse, turn things around and redeem the most difficult human problems. Resurrection power is not just an abstract force with vague possibilities, but rather a power that works directly on our addictions, character defects and defeats to transform them from weaknesses to strengths. This is the power of the cross and the presence of Christ in the life of the believer. It is what God is after in us and what He is determined to accomplish with us this side of the grave. He is doing it every day in the lives of ordinary people. This includes displaced Christians struggling with addiction to lust.

Like the Hebrew Christians of old, we Christian sex addicts are a displaced people looking for a home. Many of us have been exposed or admitted wrong-doings that have wounded our spouses, churches, friends, family and careers. We have spent significant time in recovery admitting dark and shameful secrets. We are often "ruined" for routine church life, where the sharing of needs often seems designed for "good people" making modest course corrections, a superficial and routine exercise rather than a revolutionary spiritual activity. Living in this post-deluvian world takes many adjustments for us addicts. In our dark and lonely nights, many of us have wondered, "Is it over for us? Are we beyond usefulness to God?" The answer is "Far from it." In fact, not only are we not forgotten. It is likely God can use us now in ways he could never have used us before.

Secondly, like the Hebrew Christians, we are urged to go forward and not backward in our faith.

Hebrews 10:35-39 urges us forward.

[35] So do not throw away your confidence; it will be richly rewarded. [36] You need to persevere so that when you have done the will of God, you will receive what he has promised. [37] For,

"In just a little while,
> he who is coming will come
> and will not delay."[a]

[38] And,

"But my righteous[b] one will live by faith.
> And I take no pleasure
> in the one who shrinks back."[c]

[39] But we do not belong to those who shrink back and are destroyed, but to those who have faith and are saved.

It is a natural human tendency to want to pick up the pieces of a shattered life and put them back together. But when it comes to sexually damaging behavior, many of us have learned, humanly speaking, the wisdom of Humpty Dumpty.

"All the kings horses and all the kings men
Could not put Humpty together again."

Someone said "Things go on for a long time as they do until they don't." Such is the life many of us experienced upon being exposed and thrust into a life of recovery. One of my favorite lines from the Wizard of Oz occurs when the wizard is purportedly preparing to take Dorothy back to Kansas in his lighter than air balloon. Unfortunately, Toto unties the mooring lines and the balloon slips into the air without Dorothy, much to her dismay. The wizard, who is on board, cries out, "I can't come back. I don't know how it works!" Many of us were propelled into recovery by difficult circumstances and into uncharted territory with a shorter instruction manual than the one we trashed. Having lived one way for so long, we knew little about this new life of recovery. But one thing we did learn: We are powerless to fix ourselves.

Questions flooded into our minds such as, "Will my marriage end?" We found out the answer was "Not necessarily." But, if a marriage is to survive and thrive, it must be resurrected, not resuscitated. Something new, created on a different basis, must come into being. In the wake of sexually damaging behavior, this will often mean a deeper letting go of old behavior patterns like control, self-centeredness, defensiveness, ego, resentment and other character defects. Eventually, after a period of healing, the wounded party may find that they need to work on their co-dependent or other issues as well. When this new way of living begins to take hold, both the offending and offended party will never want to return to the way things were. Liberty to live a new life will begin to be possible and even take hold.

Thirdly, Like the Hebrew Christians of old, once we realize the promise of the new life, the old will never be quite as desirable again. These believers could not go back because there was nothing to return to. But in any case, why seek a return to a "city made with hands?" The entire point of the Epistle to the Hebrews is that Jesus, the real high priest, the fulfillment of priesthood, the sacrificial system and the Temple, has ended these things as mediating activities and indispensible persons for us. He, as the great high priest, has entered the eternal sanctuary with his own sacrificial blood, poured out for us, and brought us peace with God. (Hebrews 9:12)

No doubt there was some glory in temple worship that the minds of Hebrew Christians could both recall and perhaps desire to relive. Many would sing the same Psalms, hymns and spiritual songs they had sung in temple worship. And yet God had called them away from the holy place and into this new life of adventure, into a new world of mission.

We lust and sex addicts have come face to face with our core issue, one that will be with us as our "thorn in the flesh" as long as we live. At times, we can be filled with longing for times past when we thought of things as "normal," before our damaging behavior was exposed or before we wounded those close to us. But, the truth is we were never "normal." No sinner is. And longing for a fantasy version of the past based on an outward persona is folly.

An honest assessment of ourselves brings us back to the reality of who we are today and our calling to help others who struggle as we do. From our pain has come our calling and in our moments of clarity we would not have it any other way. Our life and freedom exist in accepting that God is in our present and future. As Jesus said, "He is not God of the dead, but of the living." (Mark 12:27) We must let go of the past, which leads to another important parallel between lust addicts and these believers.

Fourthly, Like the Hebrew Christians, we will never reach perfection in this world.

[13] All these people were still living by faith when they died. They did not receive the things promised; they only saw them and welcomed them from a distance, admitting that they were foreigners and strangers on earth. [14] People who say such things show that they are looking for a country of their own. [15] If they had been thinking of the country they had left, they would have had opportunity to return. [16] Instead, they were longing for a better country—a heavenly one. Therefore God is not ashamed to be called their God, for he has prepared a city for them. (Hebrews 11:13-16)

All monuments crumble over time. Many well-built and august structures are swept away, collapse or are destroyed. Think of the statues of Lenin or Saddam Hussein. Others must be rebuilt from the ground up. It is certainly human nature to want a city, a dwelling place, an area set aside for worship. But sometimes this desire can interfere with what God is doing and so it was with these Hebrew Christians. God was asking them to lift their eyes higher to an eternal city, a heavenly country and in doing so to accept the imperfections and losses built into this life. More than this, God was asking them to see a greater purpose in the things they suffered. We will come to this theme later in Hebrews 11 and 12.

The French philosopher Simone Weil spoke of life in two parts. The first she called "creation." This is the "building phase" of life. We accumulate things, houses, careers, marriages and families. We gain degrees, travel, excel in sports or other hobbies. We gain essential experience for our callings and proficiencies. But then comes the second half of life, what she calls "de-creation," a taking away or "surrendering" if you like. In the second half of life we give things away. In some ways we suffer more and seek purpose in that very suffering. We step aside for others to take center stage. This is a natural process. We all know people who refuse to step aside, hanging onto power and attention as long as possible. We eventually suffer illness and then die. The contrast is described well in Jesus' encounter with Peter in John 21:18-19

[18] Very truly I tell you, when you were younger you dressed yourself and went where you wanted; but when you are old you will stretch out your hands, and someone else will dress you and lead you where you do not want to go."[19] Jesus said this to indicate the kind of death by which Peter would glorify God. Then he said to him, "Follow me!"

This is a passage I have returned to many times in recent years because it describes a process taking place within me. It encapsulates a desire to surrender to God's purposes in my life, even though these purposes may involve suffering. It is as if he is beckoning me to come to him and share this experience as a necessary path toward spiritual growth with him. Having spent much of my earlier years grasping at ephemeral things or attempting to stave off difficult seasons by addictive behavior, I am now learning to surrender.

If you remember, earlier Peter had asked Jesus to bid him come to him on the water. (Matthew 14:28) Instead of looking at Jesus, Peter looked down at his own feet and sank. Despite Peter's stated desire, he was not ready to look only to Jesus and let go of his fears.

Notice that it is only when Peter has first heard this prophetic utterance about his future that Jesus fully restores him by saying, "Follow me." It is as if he is saying to Peter, "This is what I really meant when I called you the first time. Can you finally, after all you and I have been through together, embrace it?" Can you allow me to "de-create you" in this life so that you may inherit what my Father has planned for you in the next?"

So much of Peter's bragging during Jesus' earthly ministry was an attempt to accumulate things he lacked, faith, humility, peace, acceptance, courage. Now he could receive them as a gift by surrendering to the path laid out for him. The man who thought it all depended on him when he asked Jesus to allow him to come to him on the water, could now surrender to the path ahead and embrace it. We will return to this passage later to discuss other recovery issues.

Here is the truth. When we understand that nothing of enduring value can truly be taken away from us, we are becoming kingdom people. Many of you might be familiar with the October 28, 1949 journal entry of Jim Elliot, the missionary to Ecuador who was speared to death by the Auca Indians in the 1950's. It reads "He is no fool who gives what he cannot keep to gain what he cannot lose." Jesus taught his disciples, "Fear not, little flock, for it is your Father's good pleasure to give you the kingdom." (Luke 12:32) So, when we finally realize that "All things are yours, [22] whether Paul or Apollos or Cephas[c] or the world or life or death or the present or the future—all are yours, [23] and you are of Christ, and Christ is of God," (I Corinthians 3:21b-22) then we will realize that the imperfections and de-creations of life are actually a necessary preparation for something better and eternal. Things that once we see, we can fully embrace without regret, shame or fear. This is the message of Hebrews and the message of recovery.

Three

Truly the hills are a delusion, the orgies on the mountains.
Truly in the LORD our God is the salvation of Israel.

JEREMIAH 3:23

"We have worshipped our way into the porn
problem and we will worship our way out."

LUKE GILKERSON, BLOGGER AND AUTHOR

Consider this portion of Hebrews 3.

⁷ So, as the Holy Spirit says:
"Today, if you hear his voice,
   ⁸ do not harden your hearts
as you did in the rebellion,
   during the time of testing in the wilderness,
⁹ where your ancestors tested and tried me,
   though for forty years they saw what I did.
¹⁰ That is why I was angry with that generation;

I said, 'Their hearts are always going astray,
and they have not known my ways.'
[11] So I declared on oath in my anger,
'They shall never enter my rest.' "[a]

[12] See to it, brothers and sisters, that none of you has a sinful, unbelieving heart that turns away from the living God. [13] But encourage one another daily, as long as it is called "Today," so that none of you may be hardened by sin's deceitfulness. [14] We have come to share in Christ, if indeed we hold our original conviction firmly to the very end. [15] As has just been said:

"Today, if you hear his voice,
do not harden your hearts
as you did in the rebellion."

[16] Who were they who heard and rebelled? Were they not all those Moses led out of Egypt? [17] And with whom was he angry for forty years? Was it not with those who sinned, whose bodies perished in the wilderness? [18] And to whom did God swear that they would never enter his rest if not to those who disobeyed? [19] So we see that they were not able to enter, because of their unbelief. (Hebrews 3:7-19)

In the Lord of the Rings, the primary negative result of Frodo's ring-bearing quest to Mordor with Samwise Gamgee is that he can no longer hear anything around him whenever the pull of the ring is near. Samwise often calls to him but Frodo is deaf because, as the ring-bearer, he is often power drunk. The ring's presence often seduces him. Nearing Mt Doom, Frodo says," I can't recall the taste of food, nor the sound of water, nor the touch of grass. I'm naked in the dark." The obsessive nature of any addiction similarly draws our attention from the varied aspects of life, its rich colors, tastes and rhythms and focuses it narrowly on the addictive substance, plunging us into isolation and darkness. For the lust addict, this is pornography or the pursuit of sexual stimuli.

A sex addict friend remarked that when he is walking down the street and a lust object (in the form of a real person) approaches, he simply cries out to Jesus "Come in." He wants Jesus to enter his soul and fill the neediness that the lust object reveals inside him. Martin Luther said, "Our sins press us to Christ." The paradoxical nature of recovery is that our very weakness is the agent of God's nearness.

In Hebrews chapter 3, there is a similar warning and appeal to hear "his voice" (7a) and not to "harden your hearts." (8a), so that you may "enter my rest." (11b) So how is a believer, saved by grace, unable to "enter his rest?"

It is not difficult to understand. When a person like me is feeding his sex addiction, the voice of God and the presence of Jesus fade. In the Return of the King, the creature Gollum, similar to Frodo, recounts his descent into The Ring's domination. "And we forgot the taste of bread, the sound of trees, the softness of the wind. We even forgot our own name." Think of the lust addict who stays up all night looking for the next porn image, forgetting to eat, sleep, bathe or prepare for work the next day. The idol, in this case lust in any form, becomes the go to functional god, no matter what the stated prior belief.

One of the realities we are faced with today is that when it comes to lust, 30-50% of clergy and evangelical Christians are like Frodo and Gollum. We have embraced a calling (a quest) of some kind. We freely admit that we are sinners saved by grace. Yet we are too often unable to hear God's voice due to the omnipresence of picture-lust. Our hearts are hardened by false gods who beckon us and as a result rest eludes us. This is why Jesus speaks so personally to every burdened soul when he says, Come to me, all who labor and are heavy laden, and I will give you rest. (Matthew 11:28). The burdens of our false gods, in the words of the 1928 Book of Common Prayer, have become "intolerable," too great to bear. One of the greatest of these burdens is the loss of God's voice.

Several years ago, before I embraced sobriety in sex addiction, which for me involved no self-sex and no pornography, I had come face to face with the possibility, at 59 years of age, that I would be a practicing sex addict for the rest of my life. Having visited the world of XXX movie theatres in the 1970's and 80's, I was well aware that these theatres were filled with grey and white haired men. Recently, a friend of mine told me that his wife had come upon an 85 year old man in an assisted living facility masturbating in front of a computer. These and other stories and first-hand accounts had convinced me without any doubt that time and age does not cure sex addiction.

I had personally made all kinds of vows and resolutions to myself at age 30, 40 and 50 that I would give up my lust-based sexual behavior. But I had failed miserably to follow through with my intentions. Then in 2009, my father died. In the aftermath of his earthly demise, my own version of a "do not harden your hearts" came to me. A voice spoke to me. "Don't kid yourself. There is now no one above you on your family tree. You are the next male to die. If you don't do something soon, you will die a practicing addict." This was indeed a restless thought.

A short time later, I watched a video from a psychologist which stated in blunt terms that there is a sickness unto death, namely a place in addiction where humanly speaking a person seems unable to return from. Hopelessness and a well-worn path combine to create spiritual inertia. (As I write these words, I think about a referral I received recently of an 80 year old retired minister caught in sexual addiction. I feared he might not call for help due to his age. So far he has not.) Whereas, God was always willing to restore, it was possible to get to a place where I might no longer believe I could be restored or wanted to be. I did not want to get to that place.

At the same time, my deafness to God's voice was becoming habitual. In 2008-2010, I was binging on internet porn, watching it sometimes 3-4 hours a day. My addiction was getting worse. At times like these, the enemy sees an opportunity to go in for the kill. But just as in AA which speaks about an alcoholic binge as an opportunity to talk to a previously resistant person, so God showed up on my behalf. Looking back, I was clearly becoming more and more miserable. I was engaging in the activity but feeling worse and worse all the time.

One day, I was watching porn at work and inadvertently printed a page of it on the centrally located office printer. Not wanting anyone to see it, I ran to the printer and shoved the piece of paper in my pocket thinking I would dispose of it later. But I forgot about it. Instead, later that night, when my wife was doing the laundry, she pulled out the paper from my pant's pocket, called me to the laundry room and asked, "What's this?"

I cannot accurately describe what happened next, but I know what I felt. It was like something let go inside me and then a distinct voice. "It's over." God always seems to speak to me in short sentences of five words or less and this was no exception. It's over? Why these words when I was in deep trouble?

It didn't matter. The trouble might be temporary but the willingness to "go to any length" to get sober for the first time entered my soul. The compulsion had somehow been given a mortal blow. I was like a man suddenly confronted with a jailer standing at an open prison door saying "In or out?" I had already made the choice. I was out in a flash. What did my heart tell me once I heard his voice? Simply that I was now willing to do whatever it took to stay sober, the indispensible drive that animates all long-term sobriety. In the next few days, I ran back to the sex addition recovery group I had walked out of years earlier, whose program I had never worked in its entirety. I started to work it full bore. I got a sponsor, started working the 12 Steps, journaling, making phone calls, doing service and eventually gathered men to sponsor. I surrendered to God and the 12 Step program. I have been sober by God's grace ever since.

"Today, if you hear his voice, do not harden your hearts as in the rebellion." (Hebrews 3:14)

I suppose I could have hardened my heart. But Jesus had met me at my point of need. He had visited me in the darkness and bondage of my soul and opened the path to freedom. I have since wondered why through many other seasons of my life, I did not find a way to surrender. I can only say I was not ready. And in recovery readiness is all.

The Hebrews 3 passage ends by saying, "...they were unable to enter in because of unbelief." The phrase to "enter in" connotes several kinds of rest. Entering into the promised land to rest from slavery and wandering. But also entering "into his gates with thanksgiving and into his courts with praise" (Ps 100:4) connotes worship, as does Psalm 24:7 with its command in temple worship to:

Lift up your heads, you gates;
>   be lifted up, you ancient doors,
>   that the King of glory may come in.

In one case, we are called to enter in. In the other, the King of Glory enters into our souls. The result is the same, intimacy, connection with Him. When I surrendered lust, he simply came in and occupied the empty space bringing peace and satisfaction.

When Jesus' death prompted the temple curtain to be torn in two, the barriers to God were taken down. Eventually the temple itself with all its walls between Jew and Gentile, men and women, priest and people came down as well. Intimacy with God and healthy intimacy with others became possible, inaugurated by Jesus's death and resurrection. This is essentially the message of:

"There is neither Jew nor Gentile, neither slave nor free, nor is there male and female, for you are all one in Christ Jesus." (Galatians 3:28) The cross, where we are all alike sinners and all alike redeemed is the great unifier of all humanity. It is at the cross when many first learn to worship, as Jesus promised the woman of Samaria they would, "in spirit and in truth," (John 4:23) freed from geographic locations.

This is what the sex addict seeks but cannot find until he or she comes face to face with Him, the true connection, and says "Come in." Not "knowing his ways," remaining stymied in "unbelief," held us captive until we experienced his gracious presence and "let go absolutely." This is what AA's have called 'the expulsive power of a new affection."

Larry Poland recounts the following story which I abridge for purposes of space. Several years ago, a high-powered Jewish couple living in Hollywood got a nasty divorce. The husband was an attorney and managed to remove his wife from the house and into an apartment. After a long day packing and moving, the wife, now all alone, finally dropped the last box onto her hallway floor and collapsed. Realizing the finality of it all, she yelled out in exasperation, "Doesn't anyone care?" As soon as she said this, a voice said, "I care." She asked "Who are you?" The voice said, "I am Jesus." She was converted on the spot. When asked later by her friends, "Why Jesus? Why not Buddha or Mohammed?" She replied, "If Buddha or Mohammed would have said, 'I care,' I would have followed them, but it was Jesus." Only God can do that. He is master of showing up in the hopeless place with his love and mercy.

This leads to the question of the role of the 12 Steps in enabling the kind of transformation we are speaking about.

The Twelve Steps themselves cannot create this experience. Rather, they are meant to illuminate and support it. This is why belief in a higher power in Step 2 precedes surrender in Step 3. It is God who keeps us sober because our addiction masks a search for him. The early AA's said, "Find God or die." But we cannot enter in before Step 2 because we have yet to believe He can take away the compulsion. Once we do, we are ready to surrender. And this principle applies whether one is Christian or not. We are all the same. Once we see this, each of us can avail ourselves of the same remedy. The door to God is open to all.

Many people wonder why the 12 Steps refer to a 'higher power." The reason is that every 12 Step program is open to anyone desiring to stop lusting, drinking, or whatever the addictive problem is. Recovery does not require prior religious belief. In fact, many people testify that previous religious belief was a barrier to recovery for them, sometimes creating a block to real honesty. Many of us grew up in homes where the culture was moralism and secrecy rather than honesty and redemption. Christianity is first caught, then taught. It is the same with recovery. When we discover God's power experientially and begin to work the 12 Steps, we can trust God, perhaps for the first time. This is a transformative power and presence which is open to all, not just to those with prior faith.

The question arises: What if none of this has happened to me? What if I cannot or have not surrendered yet? What if I am still in the grips of my addiction? This is the question of God's timing. Let's make it personal. My question is: Why did God allow my addiction to hold sway until age 59, with all of its destruction? My answer may not satisfy you but it is this: I was not ready. He had not worked his readiness in me until that time. The phrase "as long as it takes" is true in recovery as well. I cannot know how long it will take for anyone to find their bottom and let go. That is God's business. He has the whole picture. I do not.

Does this produce some outrage in you, perhaps as you look at your own addiction or that of those close to you? I don't blame you for feeling some. One of the most difficult passages in the New Testament is a familiar one. "Therefore God has mercy on whom he wants to have mercy, and he hardens whom he wants to harden." (Romans 9:18) We could even go on to fault God for allowing the children of Israel to die out in the wilderness in order to weed out the unbelief among them. But we are not God. As Isaiah says,

> "For my thoughts are not your thoughts,
>   neither are your ways my ways,"
> declares the LORD.
> ⁹ "As the heavens are higher than the earth,
>   so are my ways higher than your ways
>   and my thoughts than your thoughts. (Is. 55:8-9)

There are mysteries we cannot fully fathom and truths we have not un-packed yet. Jesus said to the disciples, "I still have many things to say to you, but you cannot bear them now." (John 16:12). If we believe God loves us, and we have so much evidence that he does, then perhaps the hidden things of God are withheld out of love. As long as we are in this world, we have the power to choose. But after we have chosen, we become servants to the things we have chosen. That we cannot change.

Four

Our Restless World: Why It Ultimately Disappoints

Unlovely, I rushed heedlessly among the lovely things thou hast made. Thou wast with me, but I was not with thee.

St. Augustine

Every saint has a past and every sinner has a future.

Oscar Wilde

Caravaggio: The Calling of St. Matthew

Look at the painting above. What do you see? Jesus is on the far right. His arm is outstretched and pointing. To whom is he pointing? No, not at the closest one. Not even at the anyone hoping he might choose them. No, Jesus points to the one way on the other side. It is Matthew, the tax collector. He is also called Levi, a man who bears the "priestly" name and is anything but. A traitor. A cheater. Despised. Please notice that Matthew is so consumed with money that he won't even look up from his counting table. But despite this and perhaps because of it, Jesus wants him to be his disciple, a follower, eventually a friend. "Him?"...one of the well-dressed men seems to be asking as he points to Matthew. Yes, him. But why?

Could it be that he was among those who were most hungry and thirsty? Did Jesus know this because of Matthew's money-grubbing occupation or did Jesus perhaps see it in his eyes? Could it be that those seated closest to Jesus were looking for nothing more than a religious conversation with an emerging messianic rabbi but that Matthew needed to find God or die? I think so. Jesus wants the hungry and thirsty people. He claimed that he was calling (picking, choosing, preferring?) those who were "sick" rather than well, "sinners" rather than "the righteous." A quick perusal of the beatitudes tells us that among other qualities, the make-up of the kingdom consists of: the spiritually poor, grieving, undistinguished people who hunger and thirst for righteousness. That is a perfect description of the sexually broken, the lust addict looking for a way out.

As we have seen, the "rest of God" has been available to humans since creation. It is memorialized in the Sabbath when God rested after he created the universe and symbolized geographically in God's promise to the Israelites to enter the promised land and find rest from their enemies. God asked them to copy him by observing their own Sabbath.

But as we read on in Hebrews, we run into a conundrum not easily resolved by looking at the text through either historical events or the eyes of religious tradition. One verse in Hebrews 4 sticks out in this regard.

"Since therefore it remains for some to enter it, and those who formerly received the good news failed to enter because of disobedience, again he appoints a certain day, "Today" saying through David not long afterward, in the words already quoted,

Today if you hear his voice,
Do not harden your hearts." (Hebrews 4:6-7.)

We might rightly ask, if someone has "formerly received the good news," how could they "fail to enter" God's rest? Is it possible for Christians on their way to heaven to fail to experience God's rest? Apparently so. The passage of course refers back to the exodus, the wilderness wanderings and the unbelief of many of the Israelites. They did not trust God enough to enter into the land of Canaan, fight the necessary battles to come, and find rest. A whole generation was forced to live in the desert before Joshua led those who believed into the place of rest. Why? Because "they were not united in faith with those who listened." (Verse 2b)

Sex addiction is a disease of restlessness. As a spiritual illness, it seeks the next high, the next person, the next experience whether it be through internet pornography or a sexual hookup with a real person. Those who practice it inevitably turn Martin Buber's I and Thou encounter into an I and "it" manipulation. People who break these boundaries often admit after the fact that their addiction is nothing less than an adventure in unreality and fantasy. It is purchasing misery, the aching inevitable consequences that always follow sexual sin. We end up using people for self-centered goals, while destroying our own connection to reality and God in the process.

The "driving force" behind sexual acting out, as indeed in all addictions is the character defects that lie "close at hand." When Jesus speaks of what "defiles a person," he mixes in the sexual and relational sins together. Character defects and sexual sin all derive from the same negative force. Because he "knew all people," (John 2:24) Jesus apparently knew about the negative, mutually reinforcing nature of character defect and lustful deeds.

"What comes out of a person is what defiles them. [21] For it is from within, out of a person's heart, that evil thoughts come—sexual immorality, theft, murder, [22] adultery, greed, malice, deceit, lewdness, envy, slander, arrogance and folly. [23] All these evils come from inside and defile a person." (Mark 7:20.)

If we ferret out the sexual sins from this list, we are left with the character defects. Unless we are willing to admit these defects and the havoc they have wreaked in our lives, become willing to surrender them and do the opposite of what they are, we will never find rest. This is why surrendering the addictive substance (Steps 1-3) must be followed by surrendering character defects (Steps 4-9) 2

In the early days of AA, the routine was simple. The alcoholic was taken "upstairs." During that time, he or she worked the first three steps. Were they truly powerless? Did they believe that God could restore them to sanity? Would they surrender to him by turning their wills and lives over to his care? Only when they were willing to take these steps and got down on their knees and prayed a prayer of surrender, were they allowed to come downstairs and join the fellowship of AA. These three steps are sometimes summarized by the statement. "I can't. God can. I think I'll let him." The individual was "in the program" now. And the way they specifically worked our their surrender in Step 3 was by working Steps 4-9.

As important and pivotal as Step 3 was, on its own it lacked specificity. The addict had to 'work out (his or her) own salvation with fear and trembling." (Philippians 2:12.) Steps 4-9 are the character action steps and include the recognition and confession of wrongs (4 and 5), detailing of specific character defects and the willingness to have God remove them (6 and 7) and being willing to make amends in appropriate ways, times and places. (8 and 9)

The 12 Steps are designed so the addict, in this case the sex addict, will begin to get off the treadmill of his or her addictive behavior, be released from their inner obsession and compulsion and begin to find rest in God. Interestingly, in the Epistle to the Hebrews, we find a similar exhortation, though it is stated in a more generalized fashion.

[11] Let us, therefore, make every effort to enter that rest, so that no one will perish by following their example of disobedience.

[12] For the word of God is alive and active. Sharper than any double-edged sword, it penetrates even to dividing soul and spirit, joints and

marrow; it judges the thoughts and attitudes of the heart. [13] Nothing in all creation is hidden from God's sight. Everything is uncovered and laid bare before the eyes of him to whom we must give account. (Hebrews 4:11-13)

Notice the passage begins with the promise of rest and ends with accountability. They go together. Like the 12 Steps, the promise of rest is strong, but it requires an action-based definitive follow through, one that never ends. We must give account to God ultimately, but to also to others in this life. The Scriptures call this "walking in the light." [7] But if we walk in the light, as he is in the light, we have fellowship with one another, and the blood of Jesus his Son cleanses us from all sin. (1 John 1:7) John is telling us that fellowship is conditional on "bringing the inside out," letting other believers know how things are really going inside us. This kind of transparent and rigorous honesty is essential for those struggling with lust. Deception has been the launching pad for our recurring problem. Truth telling on ourselves is its antidote.

A person very new to the 12 Step program recently asked me, "When does a person finish with the 12 Steps?" My reply was "Never." Indeed, they become a way of life, taking the role in our lives, not of a linear study course from which we graduate, but rather of the spokes of a circle. Any step can be employed as needed at any time. But the goal is always to "find our rest in Thee." (St. Augustine) But what kind of "rest" is this and what does it mean for us?

America's most famous shrine reflects this truth of the "rest of God" in statuary. The Lincoln Memorial is currently scheduled to undergo a thorough renovation in time for the 100th anniversary of its completion in 1922, one at which Lincoln's only surviving son Robert at age 78 was the guest of honor. Have you ever noticed that most statues of presidents and generals portray them standing or riding a horse? We have one here in Jacksonville Florida which depicts the man for whom the city is named, Andrew Jackson, mounted on his horse. But the Lincoln Memorial (below) depicts Abraham Lincoln in an unusual posture. Lincoln is seated. He is at rest. There is much symbolism in the entire memorial but I want to confine myself to the figure of Lincoln himself. Why did Daniel

Chester French depict him so? No one knows for sure but here are my thoughts. Consider them as you pond the figure of Lincoln.

Lincoln is often referred to as the "American Jesus." He was assassinated on Good Friday, April 14, 1865. The New York Times ran a piece in 2006 which said the following: "Despite the Good Friday coincidence, the Jesus parallel was not an obvious one for 19th-century Americans to make. The Protestant population, then as now, included a vigilant evangelical minority who thought that Jesus, sinless on earth, was defamed every time ordinary sinners presumed to imitate him. No mere mortal could be put beside Jesus on a moral balance scale.

But Honest Abe overwhelmed the usual evangelical reticence — by April 1865 the majority of Northerners and Southern blacks took him as no ordinary person. He had been offering his body and soul all through the war and his final sacrifice, providentially appointed for Good Friday, showed that God had surely marked him for sacred service.

At a mass assembly in Manhattan five hours after Lincoln's death, James A. Garfield — the Ohio congressman who would become the second assassinated president 16 years later — voiced the common hesitancy, then went on to claim the analogy: "It may be almost impious to say it, but it does seem that Lincoln's death parallels that of the Son of God."

We should say that Lincoln was not exactly like Jesus, the sinless Son of God and Son of Man. But certain aspects of their identities and what they accomplished are similar. Lincoln brought a divided nation together. (Ephesians 2:14). He suffered in the flesh, came from humble origins, was self-taught and was ridiculed because of his roots. Both Lincoln and Jesus worked in wood. People ridiculed the "rail splitter" as they did the "carpenter's son."

I believe Lincoln is depicted seated, sheltered from the elements, because he is "resting from his labors." In a similar fashion, Hebrews depicts Jesus "seated at the right hand of the throne of God." (Hebrews 12:2) Having said at Gettysburg that those who struggled there "died so that that nation might live," many people later believed that Lincoln too died for the nation. The Lincoln Memorial embodies this truth. Though Lincoln's left foot appears more under his body and at rest, you will notice that his right foot is placed forward, an icon of the Second Inaugural where he urges the nation to "strive on to finish the work we are in…to bind up the nations wounds." Lincoln's is not the rest of complacency. Future generations would take up his unfinished work. Jesus likewise told his disciples "greater works than these will he do, because I am going to the Father." (John 14:12) Though both of Lincoln's hands lie in the resting position, one is relaxed in repose. The other is clenched, tensed for the work that still remains. The future success of the nation Lincoln died to save clearly remains in the balance, just as the success of the Great Commission did when Jesus told his disciples to "Go therefore and make disciples of all nations. (Matthew 28:19a

Lincoln's visage communicates deep sadness reflecting the nation's present suffering during his life and death, but he also possesses a far away look that gazes off into the future, one that seems both reflective and concerned. Just so, the Epistle to the Hebrews depicts Jesus as both seated and concerned for the lives of those of us who struggle on while still in our "earthly tent." (2 Corinthians 5:1) We are told "since he always lives to make intercession for them," (Hebrews 7:25), and though his earthly work is finished, his heavenly calling continues. So both the "finished work of Christ" and Jesus' ongoing intercession for his people are visibly portrayed for us in the symbolism of the Lincoln Memorial, a powerful image that continues to stir many hearts. In fact, though I cannot prove it, I find it likely that the message of Hebrews inspired Daniel Chester French to create Lincoln's image as he did.

Notice, according to Hebrews that it takes "effort" to "enter that rest." One of the problems of evangelical Christianity today is the confusion of grace and effort. As Dallas Willard said, grace is opposed to earning. It is not opposed to effort." The emphasis on grace to the detriment of discipline is that it can sometimes lead people into an alley where there is no escape. If grace is God's answer and it has not led me out of my deepest problems, where does that leave me?

As a sex addict and a Christian, I have believed all of my life that Jesus died for my sins, that I was saved by grace alone, through faith alone and that my standing before God was completely based on what Jesus had done for me plus nothing. I was a grace man from start to finish. I still am.

Unfortunately, this bedrock truth was not decisive in lifting the sickness from my soul as I continued to practice my addiction. Now I can hear in my mind the voices of what I call the "hyper grace" people stopping me right here. They would say. "The Christian life is not about the Christian. It is about God, about Jesus and his work, not about what I am doing or not doing. It is not about my works. The sooner we stop talking about Christians and talk more about Him, the better off we will be. After all, we will never get it right in this world and focusing on our relative performance will only result in pride or shame. It's a fools game and against the gospel." I have heard this argument made in words identical to these, some of them from people who either are or have later suffered tremendous pain from their own sexual behavior. I must also say that I am sympathetic to their point of view, particularly when it emerges out of a crippling moralism that too often fosters dishonesty and despair. But God is for the alcoholic and for the sexaholic, so much so, that he has provided a way to find freedom. To say this is beside the point is to deny the life-changing provision in the gospel.

For the purposes of this book, my response to this hyper-grace message will be brief. My simple answer is that because God loves me, he wants me to be free. He wants me to begin to experience a foretaste of "the freedom of the glory of the children of God," (Romans 8:21) no matter how partial and incomplete it may be in this world. I cannot pretend that heavenly salvation is all there is or all God is concerned about. Furthermore, it is clear from Scripture that though I will never get it right perfectly in this world, God is involved at every level of my existence from predestination to justification, sanctification and glorification. (Romans 8:30) All of this means there is work going on in me and all of us that He is doing. He wants me to consciously cooperate with it. It is meaningful to note that the early AA's favorite Bible book was the Epistle of James (Faith without works is dead.) Perhaps they knew that follow-through, so problematic for the alcoholic who was constantly letting himself and other people down, was essential in order to become "happy, joyous and free."

A friend of mine who helps sex addicts says, "If you really want find help and freedom, you must embrace **task therapy** because **talk therapy** will not work." In other words, healing and change from sexually addictive behaviors will not happen by "understanding," nor by "recognizing" or "coming to terms" with my past or what motivates my behavior. These things are helpful but they will not be decisive. True lasting sobriety and recovery will only happen when I take action and do the things a recovering person does, namely attend meetings, embrace sponsorship as both sponsor and a sponsee, work the steps, surrender in the moment, serve others, keep a journal, make phone calls etc.

Today there are many Christians who are going to heaven and are saved by grace who are by their own admission bound up in sexual addiction. They are watching porn, hooking up and otherwise medicating themselves sexually through life. They are secretly miserable, fearful, resentful and isolated. I know because I was that person. How many of us have heard a sermon or teaching that goes like this: "Isn't it wonderful that no matter how many times I sin, I can receive forgiveness from the Father's hand? He is truly a God of grace and of second, third and fourth chances." Yes, that is wonderful. Thank God for it. I received it many, many times. And I still need this message! But it is only one side of the story, a story whose other side includes transformation and deliverance as well as pardon. To walk this road will likely involve pain, confession and a commitment to a program of recovery. But is worth every tear and sleepless night.

We owe those who struggle with lust more than a message of forgiveness. They have asked for forgiveness dozens, even hundreds of times. For the most part, they are grateful for that forgiveness. Make no mistake. But what they are looking for is a way out. If it exists, we would be derelict in our duty if we did not help them find it.

This brings us back to Hebrews 4 and the issue of knowing oneself. There is no recovery from addiction without "rigorous honesty," the ability to overcome a life of self-deception by walking in the light and being honest with ourselves about the true motives lying beneath our decisions and actions. But how are we to know ourselves without God? We cannot. Fortunately the "word of God" comes to our rescue. Notice in above passage, the "word of God" is both an "it" and a "him." It is both his voice and his presence, the word of God written and the Son of God given.

But what does this "word of God" accomplish for us that we cannot do for ourselves? It is first of all "living and active." A word that is living and active is a creative force. Living things move around, accomplish things, and express the very nature of their being. This is the nature of God. He is orchestrating our days, speaking to us through his creation, through the events of the day, through conversations, "God-incidents" and so on. About four months ago, I had a series of "double encounters" that could not possibly be coincidences. I heard a story about ducks on the radio, then saw some walking in front of me in the car 30 seconds later. I was listening to a biography of Alexander Hamilton, then turn on the television to a special about him. And on and on it went until it became laughable. Okay, okay, I thought. Why is this happening? Then I realized that God was simply telling me that he cared about my life, that He was putting things in order and that He was filtering the events of my life through his hands to suit his purposes. He was with me. Wasn't that Jesus's final word to his disciples before he left this world, the promise to be with them? Should we expect to see signs of his presence while we live or simply accept it on faith? I had more questions. Why should these things be happening now? Were they signs that the lust-block that had so clouded my life was dissipating as the morning fog and a clearer vision was taking its place? Whatever it was and the reasons for it, this was drawing me to him.

A similar sentiment was expressed in wonder by David.

O LORD, you have searched me and known me!
² You know when I sit down and when I rise up;
    you discern my thoughts from afar.
³ You search out my path and my lying down
    and are acquainted with all my ways.
⁴ Even before a word is on my tongue,
    behold, O LORD, you know it altogether.
⁵ You hem me in, behind and before,
    and lay your hand upon me.
⁶ Such knowledge is too wonderful for me;
    it is high; I cannot attain it. (Psalm 139: 1-6)

Hebrews 4:12 speaks powerfully about God revealing and shaping our hearts from the inside out. When he enables and frees our hearts, compulsion from the outside is removed because it becomes unnecessary. Christopher West, commenting on Pope John Paul II's Theology of the Body, explains it this way.

"This means that as a person man…can experience the objective good that fulfills him and the evil that harms him. When he does, the objective norm no longer feels imposed from the outside but wells up from within. People no longer feel forced to conform to truth. They want to conform to truth. John Paul maintains that, despite sin, an "echo" of God's original plan remains deep within the human heart. In his Theology of the Body, The Pope aims to help people peel away the layers of debris that cover the true desires so that this "echo" can resound. " (Theology of the Body Explained, p. 72)

I was experiencing this echo for the first time in a long time. Recently God's presence and intimacy became highly specific to me. My wife had received a birthday check from my nearly 91 year old mother for $166. This odd number has originated in my family as follows: Whoever has the birthday gets a check for the number of years corresponding to their birthday plus $100. Because my wife turned sixty-six, she received $166. After having received the check, we commenced a lively conversation about whether this was "income" and whether we should actually tithe it or not.

When we reached church that Sunday morning, we remembered than Bishop Joel Obetia from Uganda would be the preacher. I was scheduled to go into my 2nd and 3rd grade class as a "male presence" which I do once a month. However, today, I decided to stay in church. Bishop Obetia proceeded to tell this story:

"My wife and I decided to purchase 200 day old chickens to feed and sell. Unfortunately 34 of the chickens died, leaving us with 166 chickens. (At this point I turned and looked at my wife who still had not registered the significance.) I was going to sell them and take the money but my wife, who insists on these things, said "No, we are going to give sixteen chickens to the Lord, and so we did."

At the offertory, when our rector, Bill Driscoll, said all the loose plate offering would go to Bishop Obetia's diocese, my wife and I quickly rifled through our wallets and put the dollar bills into the offering plate. God knows are hearts and often reveals their "thoughts and intentions" seeking greater intimacy and surrender. He clearly was making it very personal that day.

Recently, I was scheduled to meet a friend at Starbucks early on a Thursday morning. The night before I had a vivid dream. An overweight black woman approached me in the dream with two chains that looked to me like a necklace in need of being connected in order to wear. She was holding both ends and asked if I could help her "connect them." The dream then faded away. The next morning I arrived at Starbucks and decided to sit outside with my friend because the day was nice. Suddenly a very nice overweight black woman approached us and said, "My car won't start. I wonder if you could help me. I have jumper cables but I need some help to connect them." It wasn't until after we helped her and she left that I remembered the dream. What was God saying? I believe He was saying simply, "I am near. I have not forgotten you. I am closer than your next breath. There is much more for you if you will listen and wait on me." I asked myself why these things seem to be happening now. Is it my age? Am I now living in the "thin places of the earth" where heaven is breaking through? I don't know. Perhaps these thin places are what is meant by the fulfillment of the Joel prophecies in Acts 2.

> "'And in the last days it shall be, God declares,
> that I will pour out my Spirit on all flesh,
> and your sons and your daughters shall prophesy,
>   and your young men shall see visions,
>   and your old men shall dream dreams;
>   [18] even on my male servants[c] and female servants
> in those days I will pour out my Spirit, and they shall prophesy.
> (Acts 2:17-18)

All I know is that in sobriety the connection between heaven and me is much stronger. Much of the blockage and resistance has been removed.

Before my surrender in July of 2010, my de facto god was lust. It occupied the immanent or near presence in my life. Lust could be called upon in times of boredom, fear, resentment, shame or a host of other emotional and spiritual tight spots. God was there but he was far away. His presence did not break through to me much because I kept him at bay. After my surrender, lust and God changed places. Lust was out there somewhere and I could still bring it in if I wanted to, but God was now in the "near place," the place of intimacy. He had waited patiently until I came to desire him. It is no coincidence that all these experiences are happening in recovery. I wonder what have I missed in my former life of addictive behavior. But all I can do now is accept my newfound freedom and make the most of it.

A big part of recovery for me has been "bringing the inside out," exhuming the dead bones of my negative self in the presence of others. We addicts have spent too much of our lives attempting to present to the world graves that were whitewashed on the outside but inside there were "'dead men's bones." (Matthew 23:27.) So what do we do with these bones that seem to follow us in some measure throughout our lives? As we leave Hebrews 4, we find direction. [14] Therefore, since we have a great high priest who has ascended into heaven,[a] Jesus the Son of God, let us hold firmly to the faith we profess. [15] For we do not have a high priest who is unable to empathize with our weaknesses, but we have one who has been tempted in every way, just as we are—yet he did not sin. [16] Let us then approach God's throne of grace with confidence, so that we may receive mercy and find grace to help us in our time of need." (Hebrews 4:14-16)

We Christians are fond of repeating the phrase, "Hate the sin. Love the sinner." But we should not press this common phrase too far. Why? Because "hating our own sin," particularly when we are living in fellowship with other Christians, whom we often perceive as not having the issues we have, can cause us to bury our struggles. Too many of us grew up in Christian families that either never talked about struggles or presumed we were paragons of virtue. Papering over the cracks in our souls, we desperately hoped for freedom before being found out. This is how universal struggles over time become "dead men's bones," festering in our own personal graveyards.

In Israel, graveyards were often out in open fields. To prevent people from tripping over them and becoming unclean by being touched by death, the graves were painted white in order to be seen in the dark or fading light.

Jesus confronts the Jewish leaders this way:

[27] "Woe to you, scribes and Pharisees, hypocrites! For you are like whitewashed tombs, which outwardly appear beautiful, but within are full of dead people's bones and all uncleanness. [28] So you also outwardly appear righteous to others, but within you are full of hypocrisy and lawlessness. (Matthew 23:27)

Jesus's judgment on the religious folks of his day was on the cover-up, the outward compensation, the idea that looking "beautiful on the outside" could obscure the reality on the inside. Jesus whole ministry, which he claimed was directed to 'sinners" and the "sick" could only operate in an atmosphere of honesty. The sticky wicket many clergy and "professional Christians" who are "paid to be good" find themselves trapped in is this: How do we be honest and bring the inside out?

In this light, these verses from Hebrews give us a different picture of Jesus's attitude to our sexual struggles. The writer of Hebrews uses the double negative. He says Jesus is "not...a high priest who is unable to empathize with our weaknesses." Why would the writer use such awkward language, unless he was attempting to overcome a stereotype, which is that the sinless Jesus is too pure to identify with our struggles? Was this the prevailing attitude? In some quarters, it likely was. The writer is in effect saying, "If you think, Jesus is too above it all and unable to sympathize with our weaknesses, boy have you got it wrong!"

He follows this with one of the most radical statements in the entire New Testament, namely that Jesus "has been tempted in every way, just as we are,-yet he did not sin." This claim is a drilling down on Hebrews 2:17 that "he had to be made like his brothers in every respect so that he might become a merciful and faithful high priest in every respect."

The first aspect of being "merciful" is that Jesus suffered similar temptations to us.

We cannot know exactly what it means to be tempted "in every way we are" but let's give it a try. This would certainly mean that Jesus was subject to sexual temptation. The passage clearly distinguishes between "temptation" and "sin." This means that Jesus certainly experienced the "pull" of sexual temptation without yielding to it. For people who encounter an attractive person, a scantily clothed person, or something online that beckons sexual desire, we can clearly understand what a "pull" is. Hebrews is telling us Jesus clearly felt this. Does this mean that Jesus felt the pull of same-sex attraction? We do not know, but it does not matter because Jesus himself in Matthew 5:27-28 has already identified "lust" as the common human sexual struggle. The particulars are irrelevant.

The modern generation has been dragged into debates about "gay marriage," "same sex attraction" and "sexual identity." They tell us that the issue of sexual attraction can be resolved by "accepting who we are." But it cannot. The real issue underlying all this is "lust and temptation," not sexual identity. Lusting and wanting to be lusted after is the universal weakness of all humankind. Hebrews asserts that Jesus was like us in our weakness and subject to temptation and therefore he can completely empathize. This is more than head knowledge or intellectual understanding. It derives precisely from experiential temptation encountered in the heat of the moment, something every one of us is subject to regardless of to whom we are attracted.

I have been greatly helped as I walk through life, to hear the words of Jesus in my spirit as I encounter various trials and temptations. The words are "I know." There is not one sexual temptation with which Jesus is unfamiliar, none that he finds shocking or strange. For not only did Jesus experience the same weakness that runs through me in his earthly life. He is so concerned about my struggle that he has passed into the very presence of God, with his own sacrificial blood and intercedes for me now so that I may I approach the "throne of grace and find mercy and grace to help in time of need." A similar truth is asserted by the Apostle Paul. [10] For if while we were enemies we were reconciled to God by the death of his Son, much more, now that we are reconciled, shall we be saved by his life. (Romans 5:10) Jesus does not just save us at the cross and then leave us to our own devices. No, Jesus brings both identification and provision. He understands our struggles because of his full humanity, makes provision because of his sinless life offered as a sacrifice, and provides moment by moment intercession before the Father. We in the church have neglected the powerful message of Jesus's continuous intercession to our spiritual peril. We will discuss it in detail shortly.

This is good news and marvelous provision for sexual sinners and everyone else. Once we admit that restlessness provoked by sinful desire is our real problem and that all our strivings to cover it up will end in failure; once we see Jesus's provision in identification, access and help, we can be drawn to surrender to him; when this happens we begin to see his desire for intimacy with us. Then we will know what it feels like to begin to walk in freedom, availing ourselves day by day of his healing presence as he joins us in all the temptations of life, one at a time, asking us to let him have them.

Five

Who Will Deliver Us?

The road to restored communion between the
sexes passes by way of the death and resurrection
of Jesus Christ. And there is no detour.

Christopher West, Theology of the Body Explained

Desire realized is sweet to the soul.

(Proverbs 13:19)

For every high priest chosen from among men is appointed to act on behalf of men in relation to God, to offer gifts and sacrifices for sins. ² He can deal gently with the ignorant and wayward, since he himself is beset with weakness. ³ Because of this he is obligated to offer sacrifice for his own sins just as he does for those of the people. ⁴ And no one takes this honor for himself, but only when called by God, just as Aaron was.

⁵ So also Christ did not exalt himself to be made a high priest, but was appointed by him who said to him,

"You are my Son,
>today I have begotten you";
[6] as he says also in another place,
"You are a priest forever,
>after the order of Melchizedek."

[7] In the days of his flesh, Jesus[a] offered up prayers and supplications, with loud cries and tears, to him who was able to save him from death, and he was heard because of his reverence. [8] Although he was a son, he learned obedience through what he suffered. [9] And being made perfect, he became the source of eternal salvation to all who obey him, [10] being designated by God a high priest after the order of Melchizedek. (Hebrews 5:1-10)

Addison's Walk is a attractivehttps://en.wikipedia.org/wiki/Trail circular footpath around a small island in the River Cherwell on the grounds of Magdalen College, Oxford. C. S. Lewis would often take walks there with friends J.R.R Tolkien, Hugo Dyson and others in the morning and evening. This repeated experience became the inspiration for the following poem Lewis wrote.

What the Bird Said Early in the Year

I heard in Addison's Walk a bird sing clear:
This year the summer will come true. This year. This year.
Winds will not strip the blossom from the apple trees
This year nor want of rain destroy the peas.
This year time's nature will no more defeat you.
Nor all the promised moments in their passing cheat you.
This time they will not lead you round and back
To Autumn, one year older, by the well worn track.
This year, this year, as all these flowers foretell,
We shall escape the circle and undo the spell.

Often deceived, yet open once again your heart,
Quick, quick, quick, quick! – the gates are drawn apart.

The themes Lewis speaks about here are directly related to the drives and desires of sexual addiction because they speak of the hope of deliverance, of a way out of the circular treadmill of the "wash, rinse, repeat" cycle of lust, acting out, shame and repeat. The human heart cries out that perhaps "this year" or "this time" things will be different. This year "summer" will actually come. This year nature, even our own, will not rob us. This time we will stop going "round and back." The poem's theme is reminiscent of the White Witch's rule over Narnia, where it is "always winter, never Christmas." At least until "Father Christmas" shows up as Narnia begins to thaw.

Part of the yearning in this poem surrounds the Christian's destiny, that we are bound for another world, not then subject to the circular sin patterns of this world, a place where all "tears and sighing" will have passed away.

"He will wipe every tear from their eyes. There will be no more death"[b] or mourning or crying or pain, for the old order of things has passed away." (Revelation 21:4.) This includes the old addictive cycle that dooms us to lust and act out. But what about while we are still living in this world? Is there a way of escape from the despair of sexual sin and addiction? Is there a way to "escape the circle and undo the spell?" Hebrews confidently says "yes." There is a way to surrender to the one who not only bore our lust but carries our weaknesses into heaven, the one who "became the source of eternal salvation." There is a way out. But how does our "great high priest" accomplish this?

Hebrews 5 indicates that Jesus is uniquely qualified to perfect the "high priest" role, one that is designed for the specific purpose of offering "gifts and sacrifices for sins." "He himself is beset with weakness." (Verse2) Jesus does this well because "he can deal gently with the ignorant and wayward." (Verse 2) How can this be? It is because Jesus took on our very nature, one that is subject to all the weaknesses of human existence, including temptation. We see from the gospels that Jesus was tired, thirsty, weary, angry, moved with compassion, tempted and otherwise subject to the experiences of our fallen world. The fact that he "did not sin" is another matter we will address later. But in chapter 5, the writer of Hebrews brings out the treasure of identification. Jesus identifies with all the challenges, weaknesses and yes sexual temptations we encounter. He is "like us in every respect" (2:17) save for committing sin. In reference to the incarnation, 4th century bishop Gregory of Nazianzen said, "What has not been assumed, has not been healed." There can be no redemption from lust unless our redeemer felt its power in his own body.

Our connection with Jesus's once for all offering is that he is our representative, subject to weakness, one who offered "loud cries and tears" (verse7) in his moments of greatest challenge, just as we would. But he was also, the perfect high priest, appointed by God (verse 5), made perfect through suffering. He "reversed the curse" of Adam by being faithful through all he suffered, becoming an "eternal high priest," one of a different order, not of the hereditary Aaronic priesthood but of Melchizedek, never dying, never needing to be replaced, one with "no beginning and no end." (Hebrews 7:3)

So to summarize, Jesus is both "priest and victim" as the hymn "Alleluia, Sing to Jesus" states. He offers himself as a sacrifice in total identification with our human condition. He could not be any more for us than his total self offering demonstrates, just as he could not be any more one with us because he took on flesh. Taking his own blood into the "true tabernacle," one "not made with hands", (Hebrews 9:11) Jesus then proceeds to make permanent and continuous intercession for you and me, the living.

But the reality is: we do not see most Christians living in the light and power of this provision. Many of us are still in "the circle," walking round and round, dreaming and even hoping for the escape Lewis's poem speaks of. Yet we remain bound. Why?

The writer of Hebrews tells us. He says "…You have become dull of hearing." (v. 11) We need someone to "teach (us) again the basic principles of the oracles of God." (v. 12). As a result, we have become "unskilled in the word of righteousness." There are a number of passages in the New Testament that refer to this common problem. Among them are I Cor. 3:1-4, 2 Peter 1:3-10.

But I, brothers,[a] could not address you as spiritual people, but as people of the flesh, as infants in Christ. [2] I fed you with milk, not solid food, for you were not ready for it. And even now you are not yet ready,[3] for you are still of the flesh. For while there is jealousy and strife among you, are you not of the flesh and behaving only in a human way?[4] For when one says, "I follow Paul," and another, "I follow Apollos," are you not being merely human? (1 Corinthians 3:1-4)

In this first case, the problem appears to be character defects exemplified by divisions lived out in competitive and "party" spirit. These defects were snuffing out the believers ability to receive deeper teaching that would enable them to surrender their rivalry, their competitive character defects that isolated them from each other and fostered competitive, prideful lives. In the Corinthian church personalities had become paramount while principles were ignored. This is always deadly in recovery groups which are designed to "place principles before personalities." In the church, our "reputations" and public personalities, often clouded in secrecy, can create strongholds that prevent true intimacy with God and others.

In the situation of 2 Peter 1:3-10, the problem is different: a severe lack of follow-through, the inability to take important action steps to build on one's faith, to incorporate the necessary building blocks to spiritual growth. Believers were failing to supplement their newfound faith with virtuous action.

[3] His divine power has granted to us all things that pertain to life and godliness, through the knowledge of him who called us to[c] his own glory and excellence,[d] [4] by which he has granted to us his precious and very great promises, so that through them you may become partakers of the divine nature, having escaped from the corruption that is in the world because of sinful desire. [5] For this very reason, make every effort to supplement your faith with virtue,[e] and virtue with knowledge, [6] and knowledge with self-control, and self-control with steadfastness, and steadfastness with godliness, [7] and godliness with brotherly affection, and brotherly affection with love. [8] For if these qualities[f] are yours and are increasing, they keep you from being ineffective or unfruitful in the knowledge of our Lord

Jesus Christ. [9] For whoever lacks these qualities is so nearsighted that he is blind, having forgotten that he was cleansed from his former sins. (2 Peter 1:3-10)

In this case, the issue challenging our spiritual growth is making sure that positive action and virtue follow on from believing, actions that will ensure a believer is "fruitful" and "effective" in their faith. This is exactly the intention and provision laid out in the 12 Steps, which become for the recovering lust addict a rule of life, a specific action plan that works every time it is employed. The 12 Steps are not the only rule of life, but evangelical Christianity's weakness has often been the lack of such a life-plan. We have already mentioned the dreaded "crisis without a process." We all need a specific path to follow in order to actualize our faith and make it real.

The 12 Steps intentionally place a priority on right action over right thinking. Rather than thinking our way into right action, which can easily get us tied into emotional and spiritual knots, we act our way into right thinking. In times of confusion, temptation and challenge, we don't get caught up in the paralysis of analysis. We simply take action and work whatever step presents itself to us in our program. More often than not, the difficulty passes or we learn to accept it as part of God's plan for us in the moment. As one wise sponsor put it, "The program works every time I choose to work it."

So if 2 Peter is correct, the problem of stunted spiritual growth among Christians is not new. In Hebrews the warning about it is directed at those who are "dull of hearing," those who are unable to 'distinguish good and evil," an exhortation aimed at those who are "unskilled in the word of righteousness." In my own experience of recovery and observing the sexual addiction recovery movement, I have noticed a common theme. Call it lethargy, confusion, or a lack of spiritual desire or understanding. For the lust addict, the addiction itself holds us in a dull cycle of inertia, blunted spiritual desire and hopelessness, a malaise that will continue as long as the addiction is practiced. This is why sobriety is necessary before recovery is possible and why the steps can only truly be worked sober. This is why

Steps 1-3 must be worked thoroughly before any others are attempted. We cannot recover while still using our addictive agent.

In an instructive Seinfeld episode, George, the neurotic, chronically unemployed friend of Jerry's, decides that he will not have sex at all. As a result of his commitment to abstinence, George becomes alert, responsible, smart and mature, the person he has always wanted to be but could not be. But as the episode moves along, Jerry detects that George has reverted back to his old self-defeating, dull, juvenile, bored and preoccupied behavior. Jerry notices this declension in George's behavior and blurts out, "You've had sex." The sex drunk who is trapped in sexually addictive behavior understands this syndrome perfectly. Whenever we engage in it, we are caught in a dull, repetitive and circular web of existence. In fact, sex drunks often cannot express themselves coherently until we move through a significant period of withdrawal. Until we let go again and surrender, we remain very sick. We must walk through the process of withdrawal again, which takes weeks and months, not days, and start over on Step 1.

The importance of surrender was crucial in early days of AA. "Ernie" described it this way. "The surrender was more than important; it was a must. Bob. E. who came to AA in February 1937, recalled that after five or six days in the hospital, 'when you had indicated you were serious, they told you to get down on your knees by the bed and say a prayer to God admitting you were powerless over alcohol and your life was unmanageable. Furthermore, you had to state that you believed in a Higher power who would return you to sanity.

There you can see the beginning of the Twelve Steps…We called it surrender. They demanded it. You couldn't go to a meeting until you did it. If by accident you didn't make it in the hospital, you had to make it in the upstairs bedroom over at the Williamses house.' " (Dr. Bob and the Good Old Timers p. 100-101)

No amount of talking, praying or resolving not to use our addictive agent again can shorten the withdrawal period. Surrender is the key. Faced with a slip, we cannot rush anything. We can only allow our lust to subside once again over time. This is why many 12 Step meetings will not allow those who have recently slipped to lead meetings or provide lead shares. They are simply too drunk to make much sense. In these circumstances, the group is not being mean or elitist. We simply do not want non-sobriety to be paraded in meetings, an ethos which could confuse or derail others. True long-term recovery means finding another way, one that lets go of addictive thinking and behavior one day at a time over time. The 12 Steps work "in sobriety." Non-sobriety returns us back to Step 1.

The writer of Hebrews, when he speaks of being "dull of hearing" is not primarily referring to people who have stopped attending corporate worship, Bible study or praying, or listening to good teaching. Instead he is referring to people who do not understand how to live a lifestyle devoted to "good' rather than "evil." They don't understand the habitual practice of righteousness to which the "word of righteousness" refers. James mentions to the same phenomenon in his epistle.

[22] Do not merely listen to the word, and so deceive yourselves. Do what it says. [23] Anyone who listens to the word but does not do what it says is like someone who looks at his face in a mirror [24] and, after looking at himself, goes away and immediately forgets what he looks like. [25] But whoever looks intently into the perfect law that gives freedom, and continues in it—not forgetting what they have heard, but doing it—they will be blessed in what they do. (James 1:22-25.)

No wonder the early 12 steppers considered James their favorite book of the Bible. Many had lived lives of "easy believism," one that minimized the actual practice of their faith, one that could not produce the "peaceful fruit of righteousness" to which Hebrews 12 refers.

What is it that the addict forgets? He or she forgets that he was cleansed from his "old sins." We forget how much trouble we invited into our lives and how miserable and desperate we were. That desperation was what got us into recovery in the first place. This is why the non-sober sex addict who is happy most of the time will find it very difficult to get sober and stay sober. For recovery, the Bible had it right.

"It is better to go to the house of mourning than to go to the house of feasting.." (Ecclesiastes 7:2) We forget that devotion to recovery means a dedication to all aspects of the program, including step work, service, sponsorship, accountability, community, journaling and prayer. We forget that righteousness is not only a gift but a calling, one that asks us to believe that freedom is a greater blessing than bondage and calls us to devote ourselves to it lest we "fall back."

Hebrews 5 ends with a rebuke for ineffective Christians based on the hearers being "dull of hearing."

[11] About this we have much to say, and it is hard to explain, since you have become dull of hearing. [12] For though by this time you ought to be teachers, you need someone to teach you again the basic principles of the oracles of God. You need milk, not solid food, [13] for everyone who lives on milk is unskilled in the word of righteousness, since he is a child. [14] But solid food is for the mature, for those who have their powers of discernment trained by constant practice to distinguish good from evil. (Hebrews 5:11-14)

We have already mentioned how in the Return of the King Frodo becomes increasingly subject to the seductive power of the ring and the evil voice of Sauron. As a result, Frodo veers dangerously off course, becomes weak, falls down and cannot remember "the taste of food" among other things. When we cannot hear the voice of God due to spiritual weakness and lethargy, we will veer off course as well. This is the condition of many Christian lust addicts today.

What is the solution? "You need milk, not solid food, for everyone who lives on milk is unskilled in the word of righteousness, since he is a child." All our addiction studies suggest a common theme. Addicts do not actually grow up while they are practicing their addiction. Our emotional age lags behind our chronological age. We retard our actual age until we surrender the addiction and become sober. No wonder the writer says he must go back to the basics. He says so because they do not understand the gospel and its basic implications. The addict must go back to Step 1. The Christian addict must understand once again the basics of his or her faith and recovery. Interestingly, the writer of Hebrews does not actually pick this theme up in the text. Does he release them to decide for themselves whether they are ready to grow up or suffer the consequences of immaturity? He does not say here. But we get a more direct message in Chapter 6.

Six

SEXUAL ADDICTION AND THE SIDELINED CHRISTIAN

"Perpetual quietness of heart. It is to have no trouble. It is never to be fretted or vexed, irritable or sore; to wonder at nothing that is done to me, to feel nothing that is done against me. It is to be at rest when nobody praises me, and when I am blamed or despised, it is to have a blessed home in myself where I can go and shut the door and kneel to my Father in secret and be at peace, as in a sea of deep calmness, when all around and about is seeming trouble."

DR BOB, ONE OF THE EARLY FOUNDERS OF AA.
(DOCTOR BOB AND THE GOOD OLD TIMERS, P. 222)

This peace and calm is often severely challenged when we become sidelined for a season. This is the experience of many a Christian leader who must step aside and devote themselves to recovery and restoration. We must remember that we lust addicts are people who have habitually attempted to bend reality to suit our own needs. Reality bursting in upon us with its painful consequences can be difficult to handle particularly in the initial stages. To become spiritually reoriented and live a new life takes time, effort, community and lots of prayer.

What does it mean to be "out of the game" for us? On the negative side, it could mean I make excuses for continuing my addictive behavior. Many Christian leaders have experienced the church as "shooting its wounded." This can lead to a season of resentment, anger, isolation and withdrawal from transparent fellowship until real forgiveness and a letting go takes place. In many cases, church authorities can make bad or hurtful decisions and the temptation to focus on their behavior instead of our own is great. Someone said to me in this phase of my life, "If you don't want to see how crazy other people are, never do anything really bad." The anger and fear our addictive revelation causes in others can be troubling. Therefore, the difficult early stages of recovery will often mean doing something very difficult, namely letting go of other peoples reactions to us. For those of us use to attempting to control other people, it can be hard to not defend ourselves. But particularly in the first stages of recovery, we must learn to let others react as they choose.

But if we are not careful, that very personal pain can drive us right back to our addictive behavior. And if lust addiction continues after heavy consequences, our Christian faith can often become ineffective in the day to day. We may start focusing on "eternity" as the only possible place of surrender or rest from our addiction. We may start presuming we can or will continue in addiction, while embracing "grace" as an excuse for behavior. There are all kinds of reasons to resent being sidelined. What I have personally discovered and others have also shared with me is that being sidelined may actually be God's greatest gift to us. This time apart to rebuild the inner self is not just necessary before we move forward. It can be a treasure we carry with us for the rest of our lives, a key element in hitting "bottom" which allows us to let go and find peace.

What Christian sexaholics must accept in order to move forward in God is that we have spiritually compromised our deepest selves. Until we can accept and own our wrongs and surrender blaming others, we will be stuck and unable to move forward. In fact, whenever we locate power outside ourselves in someone other than God, we remain captive to that person or entity. Blaming parents, spouses, either current or ex, or the church or circumstances will keep us from moving forward. Blaming others is a way of giving away our power. Forgiveness and surrender are its antidotes. No matter what others have done to us, taking responsibility for our wrongs and making amends to others for what we have done is the only way ahead. The amazing thing is that God takes care of others over time in remarkable ways. We will find many people we thought were lost to us to be forgiving people. Often as we get well, they do too. This is one reason why we discourage the "geographical cure." Many people, especially well-known Christian leaders, are tempted to move away and start over. We would encourage most to stay put, if only because in recovery, God does remarkable things in relationships. Yes, it is sometimes difficult to minister to people we have hurt. But this does not mean over time we cannot be reconciled and find renewed friendships on a person to person basis.

The theme of spiritual bankruptcy runs through Hebrews 6, a passage debated by Christians since it was written. I will not here explore the theological alternatives to interpretation. Rather, I want to unpack the spiritual condition underlying all the interpretations, for the simple reason that I believe many Christians battling lust find themselves in this place.

As mentioned previously, Christians battling lust do not help themselves by questioning their salvation, trying to get "really saved this time" nor undergo some dramatic one-time experience that will rid them once for all from their dilemma. Many of us have walked that road previously to no avail. I take the biblical assertion that Christians cannot lose their salvation at face value, notwithstanding the reality that some church members and others may admit that they have never come to Christ in the first place.

But the disturbing passage in Hebrews 6 asserts something many Christians fear about themselves, not least those who have been caught in the web of lust.

"[4] For it is impossible, in the case of those who have once been enlightened, who have tasted the heavenly gift, and have shared in the Holy Spirit, [5] and have tasted the goodness of the word of God and the powers of the age to come,[6] and then have fallen away, to restore them again to repentance, since they are crucifying once again the Son of God to their own harm and holding him up to contempt. [7] For land that has drunk the rain that often falls on it, and produces a crop useful to those for whose sake it is cultivated, receives a blessing from God. [8] But if it bears thorns and thistles, it is worthless and near to being cursed, and its end is to be burned." (Hebrews 6:4-8)

This is not just a theological passage but a deeply pastoral one as well. Many of us who struggle with lust have experienced the "goodness of the word of God and the powers of the age to come" but have found ourselves falling away from our calling, our obedience, or our inner spiritual passion. We have found ourselves bearing "thorns and thistles" and even "holding him (Jesus) up to contempt" as scoffers ridicule a faith that cannot keep us out of porn shops, internet cruising, affairs or from the deeds of lust.

The wrong response to this situation is to say, "I need to be saved again" a good paraphrase of "restore them to repentance." Those troubled by habitual lust often think, "Well, my repentance didn't work last time, so I need to do it again." Keep in mind as mentioned previously that biblical repentance is the result of spiritual transformation, not its cause. Addiction is a spiritual problem that reflects lack of true connection with God and a transparent relationship with others. True repentance follows spiritual connection. It can never produce it. I take this as the message of the Epistle to the Romans, the message of good news that rocked the world. "For the law of the Spirit of life has set you free in Christ Jesus from the law of sin and death." (Romans 8:2) In other words, our spiritual connection with Christ is of an entirely different order than the moralistic, shaming relationship set up between us and the law, one from which there is no escape, one that condemns us to return to our lust addiction again and again. This is the cycle of indulgence and blame that Jesus has made provision for, the gospel deliverance from "the well-worn track." This is why the writer proceeds to say:

[9] Though we speak in this way, yet in your case, beloved, we feel sure of better things—things that belong to salvation. [10] For God is not unjust so as to overlook your work and the love that you have shown for his name in serving the saints, as you still do. [11] And we desire each one of you to show the same earnestness to have the full assurance of hope until the end, [12] so that you may not be sluggish, but imitators of those who through faith and patience inherit the promises. (Hebrews 6:9-12)

He is able to say this precisely because his readers are not blocked or hindered by practicing their addiction. The catalyst for their service, hope and lack of sluggishness is that they have already been "set free in Christ Jesus." They know what attends salvation, namely "your work" and "the love you have shown for his name in serving the saints." In other words, they are unrestrained by the secrecy and reticence of addiction. The truly free are able to step forth to love and serve others and forbear questioning their own or other's motives in love and service. They just do it. They have "full assurance of hope until the end." Why? Partly because they no longer need to hide and practice a hindering, secret addiction. This spiritual condition allows their hope to burn bright.

If I were to say anything to any Christian still caught in this web of lies and secrecy, it would be this: It is not worth it. At the end of this sad road lies regret. Come out into the light. Tell a discreet Christian friend of your struggle. Join a 12 Step group for those who battle the same addiction you do. We cannot do this alone. There is hope and freedom and there will be future light upon your path, but only if you come out of secrecy and get help. The voice that tells you to keep it secret because you will eventually let go by yourself is a lying voice. As I write this I have received a phone call from a lust addict who has tried to fight the battle alone for the past two years. He told me over the phone, "I can't live this way anymore." He says he is now ready to join a 12 Step group and seek the help of others to recover.

Procrastination is not only the thief of time but of eternity. If you could have given it up by now on your own, you would have already done it. If you will let him, Jesus will meet you in your every day temptations and he will work his surrendering power in you. But it is up to you to come to the light or not. At some point, all lust addicts think they will be so for life. But many do recover if they can learn to surrender, become honest and walk in the light of real fellowship.

We must understand that true authentic fellowship in the body of Christ is conditional. On what? On coming to the light. "But if we walk in the light, as he is in the light, we have fellowship with one another, and the blood of Jesus his Son cleanses us from all sin." (1 John 1:7) It is far better to be known for who we are than to live a lie. The reason there is so much inauthentic fellowship today is that we are not really known for who we are. Jesus will cleanse us from all sin, but not, according to 1 John, from the sins we hide from one another. Fellowship "in the light" exists prior to being cleansed according to 1 John. Honesty with others about who we really are comes first.

James tells us, "Therefore, confess your sins to one another and pray for one another, that you may be healed." (James 5:18) Why did we ever think in the church that we could have it all together while hiding from one another? When did we think that our insides ought to match the outsides of others? Or that being a Christian meant not struggling? Nate Larkin, who wrote the popular book Samson and the Pirate Monks, was brought up to believe that Christians ought not to struggle after they come to Christ. He learned how wrong that was as he battled sex addiction. The very day we accepted these untruths was the very day we became dishonest, disconnected and unreal. Today the church has a huge lust and porn problem, largely unacknowledged and therefore not discussed. I recently attended the Set-Free Global Summit on internet pornography in Greensboro, North Carolina. The consensus among the presenters at the conference was that most pastors do not believe their church has a problem and most Christian parents don't believe their children have a problem. Both are mistaken. According to Pure-Life Ministries, the number of 18-31 year olds addicted to porn is larger than any other demographic. Isn't it about time we started helping each other? Perhaps if we learned how to help one another, we could then turn and help the rest of the world who wants help. Is the world waiting for the church to acknowledge our own porn problem so that in turn they might acknowledge theirs? This is what the Apostle Peter meant when he said this:

"For it is time for judgment to begin at the household of God; and if it begins with us, what will be the outcome for those who do not obey the gospel of God?" (1 Peter 4:7) This admonition is similar to the airline warning, "Put your own oxygen mask on first. Then you will be free to help others." In a way the world is waiting to see if our faith works. They have a right to ask us questions. Can your faith deliver you from lust and pornography? If it does, I might be interested. But if it doesn't then why would you think I might be interested in it? Why would I possibly believe your God is as powerful as you say he is? The church is on trial before a watching world like never before.

One of the Greek translations for judgment, "krisis," is "selection." (Biblehub.com/greek). In this light, Peter's admonition means that the non-Christian world is waiting to see what we will choose. Will we continue to select a lust-driven life? Or is it possible, recognizing our weakness and dependence on Jesus, for us to surrender lust one day at a time and put our trust wholly in him? The crisis or decision begins with us, not with the world. We cannot expect those who do not follow Jesus to lead the way.

Like it or not, this process begins with the people of God and we cannot underestimate the impact of our collective decision made one person at a time. If our collective answer is that we would rather indulge lust, we may witness a severe collapse of the Western church. If our answer is surrender, it could lead to a revival not seen in decades. If the power of God is seen once again in those battling lust, the world might just desire this God who slakes the hunger and thirst of the human soul. But it all begins with rigorous honesty.

The enemy is lying to us about the true meaning of our brokenness. He wants us to think it means we are finished, that God could never use us again. Today, the church has it all wrong when it comes to what we might call the "sidelined Christian." God's purpose in exposing illicit sexual behavior is not to condemn and remove us. It is to bring it to the light and restore his children, not just to a previous condition but to a condition we have never known, of peace, serenity, joy, usefulness and fulfillment we have never experienced. Far from being permanently "out of the game," or disqualified, God's purpose is complete restoration and a transparency that let's our light shine before men, not only in who we are as lust addicts but in what we have become by his mercy.

When I was sidelined years ago, a woman we did not know well brought my wife and me a needle-pointed message that said the following:

On the back was hand-written:
To Jay and Claudia, Because the promises of the Lord are true. This is for you.

On the front was stitched the following:

"I am God and there is no other.
I make known the end from the beginning.
I say: My purpose will stand.
I made you and I sustain you.
I finish what I begin.
I am he who completely restores."

I was stunned that someone would care enough to bring us this message, let alone make an artistic piece with this much creativity and detail. Through the years, these words have come back to me as a strong encouragement because of their remarkable fulfillment in our lives. His purposes do stand. The creator who made us has sustained us. We have seen that he finishes what he starts. He has completely restored us. In fact, he has restored us beyond what we were before the great collapse. No, we are not perfect. But we are growing and we are free. That is enough.

They say that broken bones now healed are even stronger than before. We are given a choice when we are wounded. We can either collapse in resentment and despair never to rise again. Or we can recognize God's restorative purposes and begin to cooperate with them. We have a choice. Hebrews 12 says,

"[12] Therefore lift your drooping hands and strengthen your weak knees, [13] and make straight paths for your feet, so that what is lame may not be put out of joint but rather be healed." God is the great restorer and he makes us the agents of restoration.

If your walls are broken in by lust addiction and its consequences, take heart from these words of Isaiah spoken to a devastated nation.

The nations shall see your righteousness,
    and all the kings your glory,
and you shall be called by a new name
    that the mouth of the LORD will give.

³ You shall be a crown of beauty in the hand of the Lord,
   and a royal diadem in the hand of your God.
⁴ You shall no more be termed Forsaken,[a]
   and your land shall no more be termed Desolate,[b]
but you shall be called My Delight Is in Her,[c]
   and your land Married;[d]
for the Lord delights in you,
   and your land shall be married.
⁵ For as a young man marries a young woman,
   so shall your sons marry you,
and as the bridegroom rejoices over the bride,
   so shall your God rejoice over you." (Isaiah 62:2-5)

This is what he will do for you. But there is more. When he does his work, he will call you into partnership and send you forth to a hurting world.

Go through, go through the gates;
   prepare the way for the people;
build up, build up the highway;
   clear it of stones;
   lift up a signal over the peoples.
¹¹ Behold, the Lord has proclaimed
   to the end of the earth:
Say to the daughter of Zion,
   "Behold, your salvation comes;
behold, his reward is with him,
   and his recompense before him."
¹² And they shall be called The Holy People,
   The Redeemed of the Lord;
and you shall be called Sought Out,
   A City Not Forsaken." (Isaiah 62: 10-12)

Once we surrender and find true recovery, we will be "sought out." Sharing in his work of restoration is an astonishing privilege, a front row seat in which to observe the power of God at work. How we participate in this will differ with each of our talents and callings. Details of this will follow later in this book. But we must first accept that not only has he not forgotten us, not only are we "not forsaken," but he desires to partner with us in reaching a hurting world. Our very vulnerability is a bridge to a waiting world, one that qualifies us to help heal hurting lives.

Seven

MORALISM AND THE GOSPEL: SURRENDERING THE INFERIOR FOR THE SUPERIOR

"How small, of all that human hearts endure,
That part which laws or kings can cause or cure.

SAMUEL JOHNSON

But where sin increased, grace increased all the more.

(ROMANS 5:20 NIV)

¹¹ Now if perfection had been attainable through the
Levitical priesthood (for under it the people received
the law), what further need would there have been for
another priest to arise after the order of Melchizedek,
rather than one named after the order of Aaron?

(HEBREWS 7:11)

M any of us grew up, if we were fortunate, in environments and families who taught us to live life morally. Our parents not only taught us right from wrong but demonstrated to us by their actions how to live a moral life. Admittedly, many parents also did not. But regardless of whether our household example was positive or otherwise, somewhere along the line we discovered cracks and fissures in the best moral examples. Perhaps, Dad got a speeding ticket or Mom had too much to drink one Saturday night. Or perhaps there was an embarrassing shouting match with a neighbor or that problem with the IRS.

Going a little deeper, maybe we discovered Dad's or an uncle's porn stash or there was that embezzlement episode or prescription drug abuse resulting in an arrest. At some point we figured out our parents were not perfect and that even they had childhood wounds, problems, character defects or even addictions.

When addictions enter the picture, whether our parent's or our own, we quickly discover that asserting morality as a remedy is itself futile. The addict quickly learns that re-affirming moral codes will not keep him or her from practicing their addiction. As previously mentioned, addictions by their very nature remove people from the directing inner moral categories of right and wrong. As Paul provocatively asserts in Romans 2 and 3, Jew and Gentile are both condemned because neither keeps the law. Being a religious Jew is no defense.

" 25 For circumcision indeed is of value if you obey the law, but if you break the law, your circumcision becomes uncircumcision." (Romans 2:25) In the presence of powerlessness to keep the law, asserting the law does no good. It is like pushing on a string. As any chronic speeder knows, speed limit signs have no connection to the vehicle accelerator. In the case of addictions, which are nothing more than habitual law-breaking, the conscience is revealed to be either voiceless or ineffective. Both are powerless over the bondage they condemn. Many practicing addicts will continually say, "I hate doing this or I don't want to do this any more." In fact, laws both human and divine can actually make things worse, provoking wrongdoing. The Apostle Paul asserts this very truth. "Now the law came in to increase the trespass..." (Romans 5:20a).

Consider a two-year old standing near a coffee table, leaning in to touch an expensive vase. When the parent says nicely, "Please don't touch that," the immediate reaction in the two-year old is of course to touch it to see what will happen. Many a lust addict who tells themselves, "I shouldn't be doing this," is actually setting themselves up to act out, creating a sore spot in their souls that virtually guarantees the next acting out incident. This is what Frank Lake called the "hardening of the oughteries" and it is deadly to the addict. Some lust addicts use the image of getting into the boxing ring with lust. Knowing lust is stronger, the whole idea is never to step over the ropes into the ring, knowing full well what the outcome will inevitably be. The law provokes a contest, one that ultimately frustrate the addict. Since our wills are captive, exerting them will only serve to facilitate our inevitable defeat.

The powerlessness of the law is illustrated by thinking of a beautiful 40-foot yacht with a rudder and steering wheel. Having an addiction is like having a broken rudder. If someone is sailing along giving instructions to the skipper and shouts "hard to port," no course correction is possible. Why? Because the rudder is broken. It does not matter how hard to port the captain steers. The yacht simply keeps drifting because its directional source of power is broken. This powerless admission is Step 1. "We admitted we were powerless over..."

The principle at stake in Hebrews 7 is similar to the Step 1 message of addiction. Remember, these Jewish believers are attempting to come to terms with why the entire sacrificial system, temple, priesthood and sacrifice, has now been abolished. Despite their former trust in it, God had brought it to an end. Jesus foretold it. "Do you see these great buildings? There will not be left here one stone upon another that will not be thrown down." (Mark 13:2) Trusting in something that will ultimately be "thrown down" is useless. Such is "the law" as a possible saving entity. It is powerless and the sooner we discover this the better.

But this provokes the larger spiritual question before us: Is there something more effective and lasting in God's provision for humans in Jesus's death, resurrection and ascension? The answer is yes.

Hebrews 7 locates this new provision in the nature of the priesthood Jesus inhabits. It is an "eternal priesthood" whose Old Testament model is Melchizedek, a man with no beginning and no end, one who predated Moses and the Aaronic priesthood, who exists prior to the law. Jesus possesses this "priesthood" because he embodies "the power of an inde-structible life." (7:16) Jesus holds this office "permanently because he con-tinues forever." (Verse 24) He has no need to "offer sacrifices daily, first for his own sins and then for those of the people" (Verse 27) Instead his sacrifice is "once for all, because he is "holy and innocent," (Verse 26) in fact God's "Son," appointed forever.

The prophet Joel foretold of God's provision for shame in the gospel. After crying out for deliverance from the shame meted to Israel out by their enemies, God promises to act, but also points forward to his full and final action in Jesus Christ. For emphasis, God states twice, "never again."

"I will repay you for the years the locusts have eaten—
    the great locust and the young locust,
    the other locusts and the locust swarm[b]—
my great army that I sent among you.
26 You will have plenty to eat, until you are full,
    and you will praise the name of the LORD your God,
    who has worked wonders for you;
never again will my people be shamed.
27 Then you will know that I am in Israel,
    that I am the LORD your God,
    and that there is no other;
never again will my people be shamed. (Joel 2:25-27)

But this shame will never be removed by human effort but only by God's action. Every Jew would identify with the Aaronic priesthood, established by God through Moses (Exodus 28). But the writer of Hebrews asserts that perfection is unattainable through the Aaronic priesthood, one literally based on human effort. For the addict, this means that no addiction was ever overcome by inner admonitions and condemnations of wrongness, in other words, by willpower. This is why the former priesthood, sacrificial system and temple had to be set aside. It was powerless to deliver. Why? Because it was based on fallen human beings, descended from one another, doing repeated acts no matter how religious, which "could not take away sins." (Hebrews 10:4)

You may well be asking yourself, "But what in the world does this have to do with my sexual struggles or those of people in my congregation? The message of Hebrews is that God has made provision for sex addiction and every other shame-based behavior, provisions that lie outside moral condemnations, either from within or without. Let's explore this eternal provision.

The first provision Jesus makes is that He bears our shame. But to understand this we must understand what shame is as it relates to lust and how it entered the world. Christopher West in commenting on John Paul II's Theology of the Body explains it this way.

"Adam was under no compulsion to satisfy mere instinct at the sight of a woman's naked beauty...This means the sight of Eve's nakedness inspired nothing but the desire to make a 'sincere gift" of himself to her. He could freely choose her because of who she was. **This is an experience far from merely succumbing to an instinctual attraction toward a generic nakedness.** (Emphasis mine) This desire and love for another person inspired by the genuine recognition of that person's authentic value-- that person's unrepeatability." (Theology of the Body Explained, p. 134)

Lust as a shame based activity wants to remove the unique personhood in favor of an interchangeable image. (This is why the internet itself can be so addictive and time-consuming, because the interchangeable images are virtually endless...my comment) John Paul describes lust this way. "Instead it grasps at the gift and instead seeks to grab it by force or manipulation. This effectively and utterly drains the gift of its meaning." This is why lust can never be satisfied, because it is looking for something that has drained all the meaning from any relationship." Pornography can never satisfy us because of the very nature of what it is and who we are. "As John Paul insists, the problem with pornography is precisely that it fails to portray everything that is human. Precisely the lack of truth about man—the whole truth about man—makes it necessary to condemn pornography... For John Paul, we could say the problem with pornography is not that it reveals too much of the person, but that it reveals too little. Indeed, it portrays the naked human body while obscuring the person." (Theology of the Body Explained, p. 290.)

The practical difficulty of this problem is vast in its implications. Most male college students today believe that marriage will cure them of their lust and porn use. Steven Arterburn has remarked how odd it is to believe that "eating wedding cake" will cure us of lust. By its very nature, lusting is a control-based, depersonalized activity which bears no resemblance to the self-giving love in marriage.

Rosaria Champagne Butterfield speaks about sexual sin in her refreshingly honest book, The Secret Thoughts of An Unlikely Convert. Referencing her speech at a Christian college, she says, "What good Christians don't realize is that sexual sin is not recreational sex gone overboard. Sexual sin is predatory. It won't be "healed" by redeeming the context or the genders... I told my audience that I think too many young Christian fornicators plan that marriage will redeem their sin. Too many young Christian masturbators plan that marriage will redeem their patterns. Too many young Christian internet pornographers think that having legitimate sex will take away their desire to have illicit sex. They're wrong. And the marriages that result from this line of thinking are dangerous places. I know, I told my audience, why over 50% of Christian marriages end in divorce: because Christians act as though marriage redeems sin. Marriage does not redeem sin. Only Jesus himself can do that." (p. 83)

Butterfield's blunt analysis was all the more encouraging to me personally because it did not, strictly speaking, emerge out of the sexual addiction recovery movement. Nevertheless, it corroborated our conviction that "lust" is the primary issue, not the behaviors it leads to. And lust can be a problem anywhere, even in the marriage bed. And those who are committed to surrendering lust will find themselves having to surrender it there too.

Marriage is no answer to lust, any more than putting the word "Christian" before the words "business" or "counseling" or "writing" ensures the character and content will reflect that word. Rather, marriage is a calling that requires putting aside and surrendering lust in order to embrace a relationship of total self-giving, one that will be seriously eroded in the presence of lust over time. In fact, the challenges of intimacy in marriage may even trigger unsurrendered lust, as couples confront normal incidences of fear, anger, conflict and alienation in the course of their marriages. So when Hebrews says,

"Let marriage be held in honor among all, and let the marriage bed be undefiled, for God will judge the sexually immoral and adulterous," there is more at stake here than adultery. If adultery alone was the writer's concern, he would have simply included the a-word without any mention of immorality. The Greek word for immorality, porneia, is far more comprehensive. The bringing into one's head of pornographic images, or past relationships, or objectifying one's spouse leading to detachment would all be covered under the defiling activities of porneia.

At this point, we might rightly ask the question, if the world is so full of these lust-driven activities, why is God being so hard on us all? Why doesn't he just grade on a curve, accept human frailty and move on? The reason is that he has created something wonderful, something beautiful, something that both enables and reflects the union of man and woman in marriage, while at the same time enhancing that union. Moreover, marriage stands as the ultimate sign of our eventual union with Jesus in the "marriage supper of the Lamb." It is God's invention and he is not going to settle for second best. And neither should we. And if we can find his purposes to overcome lust and temptation in marriage and surrender to them, we will thank him from the bottom of our hearts that we did not settle, that we did not compromise with lust.

We are engaged in an epic contest. The same one God presented to Cain. "But if you do not do what is right, sin is crouching at your door; it desires to have you, but you must rule over it." (Genesis 4:7 NIV) Either lust will "have" us or we will "rule over it" by finding freedom. There is no third way. Progressive victory over lust is the only way to find pleasure in marriage. When I realized that I must either surrender lust or it would "have me" for the rest of my life, the stakes became perfectly clear.

But to surrender lust we must first come to terms with shame. Guilt relates to what we have done. Shame relates to the reaction to it. Adam and Eve ate the forbidden fruit and were guilty of doing what God told them not to. Their shame caused them to flee from God and hide. Despite the fact that we live in a culture defiled by sexual shame of all kinds, causing us to deny our true selves and hide from God and others, we were never meant to bear shame. There was no shame in the garden in Genesis 1 and 2 and there will be none in the new heaven and the new earth. What about in between? In his once for all sacrifice, Jesus has born shame for all time for you and me. There is no repeated sacrifice, no ritual or additional good work necessary to take away our shame. Jesus has made full provision. A peek ahead in Hebrews tells us how.

Therefore, since we are surrounded by so great a cloud of witnesses, let us also lay aside every weight, and sin which clings so closely, and let us run with endurance the race that is set before us, [2] looking to Jesus, the founder and perfecter of our faith, who for the joy that was set before him endured the cross, despising the shame, and is seated at the right hand of the throne of God. (Hebrews 12:1-2)

But whose shame is the writer talking about, Jesus's or ours? It could not be Jesus's shame. He possesses none of his own. Because he is sinless, Jesus is innocent of any hint of self-generated shame, even while bearing ours on the cross. The reason he could "despise the shame" was that he knew he was not hanging on the cross for his own sins and wrongs, but for ours. Jesus's own relationship to shame is explained for us in Isaiah 53.

> yet we esteemed him stricken,
>   smitten by God, and afflicted. (Isaiah 53:4b)

If we had happened by on that first Good Friday, we might have "esteemed" or understood Jesus to be enduring nothing more than Roman justice. Though crucifixion was harsh, we would have assumed him guilty, as Isaiah intimates, that God, or at least the powers that be were meting out just punishment. We would have assumed, as many in the crowd did, that the shame placed on Jesus was his own and was therefore justified. The "honorable thief" even pronounced the "guilty" verdict upon himself, justifying the sentence upon the two men crucified with Jesus. Speaking to the other thief, he said,

"Do you not fear God, since you are under the same sentence of condemnation? ⁴¹ And we indeed justly, for we are receiving the due reward of our deeds; but this man (Jesus) has done nothing wrong." (Luke 23:41.)

Many others in the crowd also mocked Jesus because of his divine claims.

²⁹ And those who passed by derided him, wagging their heads and saying, "Aha! You who would destroy the temple and rebuild it in three days,³⁰ save yourself, and come down from the cross!" ³¹ So also the chief priests with the scribes mocked him to one another, saying, "He saved others; he cannot save himself. ³² Let the Christ, the King of Israel, come down now from the cross that we may see and believe." (Mark 15:29-32)

But suddenly Isaiah shifts his tone and proclaims another alternative to the pathetic and excruciating scene in his mind's eye, namely that this suffering servant, against all first impressions and visuals, is not, in fact, dying for his own sins but for those of others. The next sentence is without doubt the most significant "but" in the entire Bible.

But he was pierced for our transgressions;
    he was crushed for our iniquities; upon him was the chastisement that brought us peace, and with his wounds we are healed.
⁶ All we like sheep have gone astray;
    we have turned—every one—to his own way;
and the LORD has laid on him
    the iniquity of us all. (Isaiah 53:5-6)

In our permissive age, we often think that sin can simply be forgotten and we can just move on. But someone always pays for sin. Always. A just God has set up the universe and human existence this way. Perhaps this is why when our character defects trouble us, we can have a great desire to shift the blame onto someone else. Just as Adam blamed Eve, our defects are so difficult for us to bear that we will "blame shift" or "shame shift" our wrongs onto others. "It was really his or her fault that I feel this way or did what I did." In fact, my own desire to focus on another's wrongs is a way for me to attempt to find temporary but ultimately ineffective relief from my own misdeeds without going through the pain of admitting them. Until I admitted that my own fault finding was really about me, I could not truly recover inside. Until I am willing to admit the truth about myself and allow the one sin-bearer to bear my wrongs, I will find no true and lasting relief, only suppression of the truth which leads to unrighteousness. This is the great theme of Romans chapter 1.

Adam Smith wrote about the difficulty of examining our own wrongs in The Theory of Moral Sentiments (1759). "It is so disagreeable to think ill of ourselves, that we often purposely turn away our view from those circumstances which might render that judgment unfavorable...Rather than see our own behavior under so disagreeable an aspect, we too often, foolishly and weakly, endeavor to exasperate anew those unjust passions which had formerly misled us; we endeavor by artifice to awaken our old hatreds, irritate afresh our almost forgotten resentments...This self-deceit, this fatal weakness of mankind, is the source of half the disorders of human life. If we saw ourselves in the light in which others see us, or in which they would see us if they knew all, a reformation would generally be unavoidable. We could not otherwise endure the sight." (Quoted in Notable and Quotable, The Wall Street Journal, p. A11, may 11, 2016)

But what about paying for my wrongs? Payment might occur through continuing mental anguish, lack of forgiveness, guilt, resentment, estrangement and a whole host of other consequences. Sometimes, the wages of wrongdoing can be delayed for decades or even for this life. But someone always pays the price in the end. Heaven and hell, of course, are the ultimate place of rewards and punishments, the final tributes to both human freedom and the God who puts all things right in the end. The great good news of the gospel is that the God of the universe has come to bear my unbearable wrongs. He offers to come and take the burden away if I will simply let him bear it, freeing me to love and give to others.

The night I told my wife about my sexual betrayal, the truth and consequences came "out of the blue" for her. On this night in 1993, I wanted to feel better. I wanted to "get this off my chest." I wanted to move forward and the only way I could do it was to make a clean breast of it. But someone had to pay. And so I made her pay. My unburdening burdened her. The load I was carrying fell upon her. Its no use denying it. This is the way creation is designed.

As I sat in our living room, I took my misdeeds and "laid them on her." She was spiritually and emotionally "crushed for my iniquities." And that night and in the days and weeks that followed, my wife paid dearly and excruciatingly. I never truly understood what it meant for Jesus to die for my sins until that night and the days that followed.

Now think of Jesus, righteous in a way none of us has ever dreamed of being, taking on himself the sin of the world. Not just the sin of his town or area or nation. For comparison of the mental anguish of bearing one small town's sins, read The Lottery by Shirley Jackson. But this was the sin, the wrong-doing and wrong-being of all humanity, since the beginning of time to the end of time, a massive crushing load of darkness, filth, guilt and shame. This was not just a physical weight but more importantly a spiritual crushing beyond human comprehension. In taking this burden, Jesus was compelled to experience something he never had known before, separation from his father." My God, my God, why have you forsaken me?" (Mathew 27:46) It defined "the cup" he surrendered to drink in the Garden of Gethsemane, an act which meant total separation from his father. It crushed him in a way we can never fully absorb.

In light of this crushing blow, I find it remarkable that in the language of the Epistle to the Hebrews, Jesus actually despised his own shame, refusing to embrace his own guilt. In modern terms, he never "bought into" the belief that he deserved his punishment. Perhaps this is why he could say, "For this reason the Father loves me, because I lay down my life that I may take it up again. No one takes it from me, but I lay it down of my own accord. I have authority to lay it down, and I have authority to take it up again." (John 10:17-18) Perhaps this is why he was fully able to focus on others, forgiving his mockers, torturers and crucifiers, giving hope to the repentant thief and making provision for his mother and the Apostle John. Yet, at the same time, as the Apostle Peter expressed it, "[24] He himself bore our sins in his body on the tree, that we might die to sin and live to righteousness. By his wounds you have been healed. [25] For you were straying like sheep, but have now returned to the Shepherd and Overseer of your souls." Exhausting the penalty, Jesus took into himself for all time the shame of our lust and sin.

2 Corinthians 5:21 expresses this idea in even starker terms, asserting that Jesus so identified with our plight that he "became sin for us, that we might become the righteousness of God." Our sin, so hidden and dressed up in our modern age, was publicly exposed on the cross for what it was and yet by the same act, we are put right with God for eternity as a free gift.

What does this mean now for our secret sins? If you think that Jesus somehow cannot handle your secret lust, remember that he already has taken it to the cross and into himself. He knows the temptation of lust for himself and what it is doing to us now. He knew the consequences of embracing it on the cross. But the one thing he cannot do is compel us to surrender it to him. But because he loves us so completely and deeply, he does invite us to do so. This is why he came. As Jesus said, "All that the Father gives me will come to me, and whoever comes to me I will never cast out." (John 6:37)

When we meet someone who is disheveled in appearance we often say they "look like hell." When Jesus hung on the cross we could say "he looked like sin." The cross is what the consequences of sin look like. The cross is an outward display of the inner presence of shame. Jesus brought the inside of humanity out and put it on public display. This is what the exhausted, tired, lonely porn addict, bereft of hope, looks like. Lust and all the other powers of this world were exposed. "And having disarmed the powers and authorities, he made a public spectacle of them, triumphing over them by the cross." (Colossians 2:15) But these consequences were ours, not his.

You see Jesus awareness that he was on the cross due to our shame and not his own gave him the power to bear ours completely out of love. Have you ever wondered why someone hanging on a cross could possibly say, "Father forgive them for they know not what they do?" These are the words of someone without resentment or anger, free to care for the souls of even the ones putting him to death, rather than engaging in the character defects of fallen men. The shame Jesus bore was all ours and none his. And because he is risen, ascended and interceding for us before the father's throne, this means there is an eternal, unbreakable connection with what Jesus accomplished for us at the cross and what we experience in the here and now.

For those who struggle with lust, as contrary as it might seem, the proper place for our lust is in the bosom of the Lust-Bearer, rather than in our own hearts. Jesus came to bear it and to take it away, provided we are willing to give it to him. Someone once said, "The problem with a living sacrifice is that it keeps crawling off the alter." This is the price of freedom. Because we humans are free, our response to the atonement is often half-hearted or incomplete surrender. But once we see that Jesus will take and bear our lust away, once we have reached the place where we want to be free of it, we can actually give it to him and experience him taking it, even in the moment it occurs.

Why don't we surrender? St. Augustine, when contemplating his own lust prayed, "Heal me Lord, but not yet." Our problem is we don't want to let Jesus take our sins. We want to hold onto them to see if there is any fascination left. The lust addict often wants to return to his folly "just to see if there is anything there" or "just to find out if there is anything I shouldn't be looking at." For us this is evidence of trying to 'control and enjoy" lust. Another dead end strategy is attempting to bear the brunt of lust ourselves by punishing ourselves. Sometimes, we even beat ourselves up morally and spiritually, perversely paving the way for our next acting out episode. We figure if we feel bad enough now, we are entitled to feel good later. This is the vicious cycle of desire and blame which defines the defeated addict. But we do have a choice. We can surrender our lust to him and let him bear it away or we can hang on and try to manage it ourselves. When I ask myself how managing it myself has worked for me, my honest examination of the record returns the verdict: Not well. Control is my problem, not the solution.

The same question might have been asked of these Hebrew Christians. You are mourning for the temple, the priesthood and the familiarity of temple sacrifice. You grew up with it and it was a big part of your life for many years. But did any of those things really take away your sins? Did they stop you from indulging your addictions? Did they deliver you from the wash, rinse, repeat cycle of your life? Their answers must be: No, no and no.

The second provision Jesus gives is the power of an indestructible life. (Verse 15)

[15] This becomes even more evident when another priest arises in the likeness of Melchizedek, [16] who has become a priest, not on the basis of a legal requirement concerning bodily descent, but by the power of an indestructible life. [17] For it is witnessed of him,

> "You are a priest forever,
> after the order of Melchizedek." Hebrews 7:15

The Aaronic priesthood was handed down father to son. The law required it, but this law guaranteed that fallen mortals would repeatedly occupy the office. This is not a recipe for transformation, but rather for congenital, inherited problems and addictions. We cannot blame our families for our addictions. But we can look back and see some seeds being sown that produced a harvest in our own lives. Every "family system" has this inheritance and the Aaronic priesthood was no exception. Neither are the sons and daughters of Adam and Eve.

But Jesus's "indestructible life" has the power to spin us out of the orbit of family inheritance and religious or sexual ritual. His life can never be diminished, ended or destroyed. Our weakness, rather than handed down or continued endlessly, can be perfected in his strength. (2 Cor. 12:9) The power is not in us. It is in Him. But in order to remain healthy, we must surrender our will and our life to him on a daily basis. The provision of the daily bread of his presence empowers the discipleship of "daily" cross-bearing, resulting in acts of daily surrender. Jesus's indestructible life must be called upon every day. This is the consistent message of the New Testament for fallen humans awaiting their perfection in heaven.

But if you are like me, this surrender is easy to affirm intellectually but difficult practically. For example, my default position when faced with either a lust temptation or an overwhelming character defect of control or resentment is to attempt to handle it myself. My inner disposition says "try to be strong." This is an ill-advised strategy which can often end badly. Why? Because what happens is either a further exerting of a corrupt will on the one hand or a lying attitude of pretending to be strong in the presence of evident weakness. My former teacher Frank Lake would often speak of "blessed immediacy" in this regard. "Here and now, I and thou, not why but how?" What did he mean? I believe he meant that in every circumstance, relationships and their attendant emotions are paramount. In terms of my relationship with God, I must be honest about the real struggle, the "how I am doing" part of life. If I am struggling with lust or other character defects, acknowledging the honest "how" gives me the "get out of jail free card" of surrendering in the moment to God's presence, the one who will bear my lust away or admit my wrongs to him or others. Alternatively, I can draw on the fellowship of recovery (Jesus with skin on) and make a phone call to surrender to a brother.

Let's say I have a resentment against someone with the result that I want to change their behavior. I will be tempted to go up to them or send them an unsolicited e-mail attempting to show them how changing the way they do things will help them to "do it better." The ostensible reason I believe I am doing this is altruistic, but the underlying reason is to show my "innate superiority." It is pure character defect. After continuously shining light on this blind spot, I am now learning to surrender all these instincts to Jesus until and unless the person asks for my help. Warning:

They almost never do. The negative force in me which God wants to take away is what is really going on here.

What about pretending to be strong? I did this for most of my first 42 years of life when my life suddenly crashed under the accumulated weight of lust addiction, Afterward, someone wisely said to me, "You now know how vulnerable you were all along but didn't know it." What did my purported strength do to me? It got me into situations of all kinds that my ego demanded, but in hindsight these events were driven by either fear or pride. Because I could not admit my weakness and seek help, I got in over my head. Skirting the edge propelled by adrenaline, in order to medicate difficult emotions, made me not only risk my own well-being but also put my marriage and family in danger as well.

After David had sinned with Bathsheba, he wrote, "Behold, you delight in truth in the inward being, and you teach me wisdom in the secret heart." (Psalm 51:6). David learned that "rigorous honesty" means allowing God's Holy Spirit to search our motives to learn how we should proceed. Alternatively, believing we are "bullet-proof" can lead us to wander into deadly crossfire.

Part of rigorous honesty is speaking honestly with others, what 12 steppers know as "bringing the inside out." Individual self examination will never completely do the trick. Alone, we simply possess too many blind spots or repressed feelings. Not only were we never meant to bear lust apart from Jesus. We were never meant to bear it apart from others. I have personally benefitted from a Daily Sobriety Renewal, a simple battery of shared questions with one other person in recovery. These questions, which bring a daily dose of reality and honesty, act as sunlight on motives, thoughts, intensions and actions. The DSR keeps accounts short and recovery fresh. The format is readily available on the internet under Daily Sobriety Renewal.

Group honesty plays its part as well. In a recovery group setting, we hear of the struggles, temptations, problems, and difficulties of others.

These are shared in the "I" form, not the "you" or "we" form. We can only speak for ourselves. There are no lectures or principles handed down in group sharing, only the "experience strength and hope" of others. In many a meeting I have listened to the struggles of others and said to myself, "This struggle is mine too." I have found deep identification and practical help as someone brings the inside out, even out of the mouth of the most raw newcomer to recovery. A friend of mine quotes a priest of 45 years who is in recovery. The priest said, "I cannot tell you one confession I heard in 45 years. But I can tell you this. We are all the same."

I have shared my own struggles and found that my own shameful thoughts and actions were in fact common to humanity. I have been able to cease thinking of myself as "special," either in a positive or negative sense, but rather simply bundled up with others in the journey of life. My own history tells me that I have spent many years trying to prove I was stronger, faster, smarter and more capable than others. This only produced misery and isolation. Now that I have accepted how wounded and fallen I am, intimate fellowship and belonging is mine. This is the power and community of recovery meetings and there simply is no substitute for it. Individualistic recovery like individual Christianity leads to the slippery slope and we must resist it with every fiber of our being. This is why clergy, often alone and apart, struggle so much in the area of lust. When we open up in the right setting, much of our addictive thinking and behavior starts to slip away.

The third thing the writer asserts is in Hebrews 7 is that Jesus brings lives to make intercession for us before the Father.

Consequently, he is able to save to the uttermost those who draw near to God through him, since he always lives to make intercession for them. (Hebrews 7:25)

We often ask the question when finding out what makes another tick,, "What do you live for?" This question usually refers to passion, interest and time spent. We all have activities that we live for and thrive doing. Hebrews tells us that Jesus "lives to make intercession." This is what interests him and what he longs to do. He is our divine intercessor, pleading before the father in our time of need. It is as if he is saying "Don't deprive me of what I am really good at by trying to manage it yourself. Give it to me." I have found this to be an enormous comfort when enduring difficult and trying times. Jesus, far from being shocked and dismayed when I run into trouble, understands and is ready to help. Specifically he will take what I cannot handle, including lust and difficult situations and take them from me, in the very moment as long as I am willing to give them to him. It works every time I am willing to surrender to him.

How is it possible to send lust away? We have an Old Testament model in the scapegoat. Directly after making atonement in the "holy place," Aaron was to do the following:

[20] "And when he has made an end of atoning for the Holy Place and the tent of meeting and the altar, he shall present the live goat. [21] And Aaron shall lay both his hands on the head of the live goat, and confess over it all the iniquities of the people of Israel, and all their transgressions, all their sins. And he shall put them on the head of the goat and send it away into the wilderness by the hand of a man who is in readiness. [22] The goat shall bear all their iniquities on itself to a remote area, and he shall let the goat go free in the wilderness." (Leviticus 16:20-22)

Notice the language. The sins were to be "put on the head of the goat and send it away into the wilderness." This substitute for sin is a type of Christ's sacrifice. We are to place our sins on his head so that he might take them away. "Oh Sacred Head Sore Wounded." It does no good for sin to be forgiven and atoned for if it is not "sent away." How many times has a lust situation occurred and there has been some sense that it has been "surrendered" only to return, too soon for comfort. How many times have we not acted out only to have the lust return an hour later or the same day? If we are honest, this is a very real problem. The answer is that Jesus not only promises to bear our lust. He also promises that we can "send it away," through him. Because I am human, this may require multiple and repeated sendings/surrenders. But this is not because he is unwilling or unable to take it the first time. It is because I am not willing to let go of it.

My experience is that if I am willing to make as many sendings/surrenders as it takes, Jesus will always take them away. He has never failed to do this.

The necessity of repeated surrender is demonstrated in The Two Towers. The divided personality Gollum/Smeagol has this conversation within himself.

> Master looks after us now. We don't need you anymore.
> *Gollum*: What?
> *Smeagol*: Leave now, and never come back!
> *Gollum*: No!
> *Smeagol*: [*stronger and firmer*] Leave now, and never come back!
> [*Gollum snarls in frustration*]
> *Smeagol*: LEAVE! NOW! AND NEVER COME BACK!
> [*Gollum is silent; Smeagol waits*]
> *Smeagol*: [*looks around; then begins galumphing around with joy*] We told him to go away... and away he goes, Precious! Gone, gone, gone! Smeagol is free! (IMDB.com)

But we know what happens. Gollum does come back and eventually does Smeagol in. This is why surrender must become a lifestyle that is never completed in this world. We never move beyond it because the very act of surrender is key to our relationship with Jesus, just as his surrender was key in his relationship with the Father. I plan on surrendering on my death bed because God has shown me how necessary doing it is to remaining free.

Jesus is our scapegoat. He not only "bears" our sin. He bears it away. We cannot simply rest in the "finished work of Christ." We must participate in the ongoing intercession of Jesus by giving him moment by moment the things we cannot bear. Every time we ask him to bear our lust away, he will do it. But we must let go and let him handle what we were never meant to bear by ourselves.

The prayer of immediacy in the heat of temptation might go like this. "Jesus, I cannot handle ____. I surrender it to you. I thank you that you are my lust-bearer. (Or resentment or fear or....) So I give it to you now.

I thank you for taking it and bearing it away from me. I now leave it with you to handle.

Please protect me from its return as I go on about my day. In your name I pray. Amen. Repeat as necessary. In the years of my sobriety, I have had to say this kind of prayer as many as seventeen times surrounding one incident. It has never not worked, and I believe it will as long as I am willing.

Seven

*The LORD is near to the brokenhearted
and saves the crushed in spirit.*

(PSALM 34:18)

*Therefore he is able to save completely those who come to God
through him, because he always lives to intercede for them.*

(HEBREWS 7:25 NIV)

Today we Christians are being challenged by a world-changing presence that is even more significant than the invention of writing or moveable type. The first invention allowed man to communicate in visible words while the second allowed us to communicate by distribution of books and other written documents. But the third, namely the internet, has given us instant communication around the globe, regardless of one's ability to read or write. Unlike radio and television, much of it is on-demand. Books, articles and videos will continue to be produced from now until the end of time about how the internet has changed our world, but one thing is abundantly clear. Instant connection is here to stay and has changed much about human interest, capabilities and drives, as well as how we spend our time.

One of the drives that has surfaced in the internet age is the drive for "connection." Many of these connections are made with wires or the much preferred "wireless." But regardless, we live in a connected world and the kinds of connections we have with people are crucial. We now possess the ability to fritter our time away surfing the web or indulging our appetites, or we can use internet connections for noble purposes or even to deepen our more authentic, off-line relationships. Connection seems to be king these days. But connection without character can be dangerous and character is being tested as never before.

We might well ask ourselves as Christians, where does our connection with Jesus stand in a hyper-connected world? Think about it. We have the ultimate connection in the universe, one that does not disappoint or fail us, one available to us at any moment, when we are with family members, or moved by art, music or a wow-filled sunset, in a time of deep challenge, and even on our deathbed and beyond. But if you asked the average Christian about their connection with Jesus, they might immediately speak about a formalized time spent in prayer or describe some abstruse theological truth. The idea of making a real-time, saving connection with him is harder to apprehend, more difficult to describe and most importantly often not made. Childhood pain and repression often block the way to this kind of connection with him. I believe it is a significant reason lust looms larger as the ultimate false connection. Lust images and connections are simply more omnipresent in an internet world, more insistent and more difficult to turn away from. How important must it be then to explore our connection with Jesus himself.

Chapter 8 of the Epistle to the Hebrews cuts right through our modern pre-occupation and formalized theology to answer the question: What is Jesus doing now?

Something to Offer

"Now the point in what we are saying is this: we have such a high priest, one who is seated at the right hand of the throne of the Majesty in heaven, [2] a minister in the holy places, in the true tent[a] that the Lord set up, not man.[3] For every high priest is appointed to offer gifts and sacrifices; thus it is necessary for this priest also to have something to offer. [4] Now if he were on earth, he would not be a priest at all, since there are priests who offer gifts according to the law." (Hebrews 8:1-4)

Notice that the word "offer" appears three times in describing the heavenly ministry of Jesus. This is what priests do and Jesus high priestly ministry is no exception. Despite the fact that his heavenly ministry is of a different order since he is not offering gifts "according to the law," (ie the blood of bulls and goats) the entire focus is what he is doing for our benefit, to provide something for us. The writer tells us that "it is necessary for this priest to have something to offer," just as his earthly counterparts must. So even though Jesus occupies a heavenly priesthood, he still resembles the earthly one in the matter of having something to offer.

The things Jesus offered once for all are made clear throughout Hebrews, himself (7:27), his own blood (9:12) and body. (10:10) He has offered these real gifts, not the "copy and a shadow of the heavenly things." (v.5.) He offered them not in a temple made with hands but in the true temple, in heaven. This will be more starkly stated in Chapter 9. Why did Jesus make these particular offerings? It is because he has established a new covenant in and with his blood. The evidence of this is the important prophecy of Jeremiah 31:31, which the writer quotes at length.

> "Behold, the days are coming, declares the Lord,
>   when I will establish a new covenant with the house of Israel
>   and with the house of Judah,
> [9] not like the covenant that I made with their fathers
>   on the day when I took them by the hand to bring them out of
> the land of Egypt.
> For they did not continue in my covenant,

and so I showed no concern for them, declares the Lord.
10 For this is the covenant that I will make with the house of
Israel
    after those days, declares the Lord:
I will put my laws into their minds,
    and write them on their hearts,
and I will be their God,
    and they shall be my people.
11 And they shall not teach, each one his neighbor
    and each one his brother, saying, 'Know the Lord,'
for they shall all know me,
    from the least of them to the greatest.
12 For I will be merciful toward their iniquities,
    and I will remember their sins no more." (Hebrews 8:8-12)

Why did God go to such lengths to procure this covenant? There are many reasons, but Hebrews tells an important one.

"But as it is, Christ[b] has obtained a ministry that is as much more excellent than the old as the covenant he mediates is better, since it is enacted on better promises." (Hebrews 8:6)

But what exactly are these promises? They are set forth in the quoted Jeremiah passage. Jesus is the mediator, the go-between, of a new covenant, a "much more excellent" one. Why? Because it is "enacted on better promises." God says, "I will put my laws into their minds and write them on their hearts." This will be an inside job. No more stone tablets and even stonier hearts. An inner desire to walk according to his ways will characterize God's people. They will cease to "fight anything or anyone." They will embrace his ways from within. Let me be blunt. Addiction inhibits spiritual desire. When addictive habits are surrendered, true spiritual desire returns over time. I have seen it repeatedly, in my own life and many others. This is why finding a way to surrender lust for those who struggle should be our number one spiritual priority. Once this happens, everything, and I mean everything, will begin to fall into place.

Secondly, we will not be compelled to rely on special teachers for our knowledge. In today's church, there is a lot of running after famous or well-known speakers, writers, seminar-leaders and the like. But Jeremiah says the inner source of God's presence, the Holy Spirit empowering God's word will spread the knowledge of Him throughout the community of the faithful. This promise was certainly fulfilled in the coming of the Holy Spirit in Acts 2. "...we hear them telling in our own tongue the mighty works of God." The teaching and understanding will not be inaccessible, remote or technical in nature. "No, the word is very near you; it is in your mouth and in your heart so you may obey it." (Deut. 30:14) The desperate search for a magic pill will cease. We will be like David who "... strengthened himself in the LORD his God." (1 Samuel 30:6)

Finally, there will be a permanent provision for sin. No more wash, rinse, repeat. No more repetitious and ineffective sacrifices. "I will be merciful toward their iniquities and I will remember their sins no more." (Verse 12) What troubles God's people today? Many things, but the memory of our sins, unfaithfulness and outright rebellion can cause us grief. Can we ever get beyond these things? When I went through my darkest moments, an older priest whom I believe knew of which he spoke said to me, "The hardest person to forgive is yourself." Many people cannot forgive themselves, let alone ask for God's forgiveness. Will we simply take our guilt to our grave?

The good news is that we don't have to. He says "I will remember their sins no more." He has placed our sins in the deepest sea and put up a sign: "No fishing." Why is this? It is because, "Mercy triumphs over judgment." (James 2:13b) Have you noticed that God has not given back to you according to your sins but has demonstrated mercy again and again? We have received mercy at the cross. Our sins have been covered, once for all. And the light of that mercy extends across time into the many challenges of our lives both small and great. It continues before the very throne of God in this moment, where Jesus intercedes for us. Therefore, we are encouraged to "with confidence draw near to the throne of grace, that we may receive mercy and find grace to help in time of need." (Hebrews 4:16b)

But there is another sense of mercy echoed in these verses. It is the provision of shared experience with the Son of Man. Jesus knows what we have been through. He has been "tempted in every way as we are." (Hebrews 4:15.) And as we will learn, he is willing to go to battle for us in our present struggles both in the crucible of our immediate experience and before the father. This is the great and powerful truth of Jesus constant availability for us who believe.

This direct experience is described in Ron J's powerful book, Impossible Joy.

" I pull into the store down the street to make a phone call. Suddenly in the corner of my eye I see the image of a woman at the bus stop. There's something about the figure and body language that wants to grab me, a powerful magnetic force pulling at the center of my soul...I want to look and connect. The memory of that past encounter is the most overpowering trigger for my lust. I am a goner! The compulsion to take that first look is irresistible. I know that I must look—and "drink." I'll die if I don't.

But I don't. **Something intervenes within me.** (Emphasis mine) As I go on my way to the telephone, there's a lingering sadness for not taking that look...But then, in what has come to be my new pattern of reaction, I lift my head upward to my Lord and God and say, "You see that my heart really wants to lust; come be victorious over my lust.. I thank Him for the trial and thank Him for the victory. And as I am making this surrender, I still have the craving and feel great loss. I don't want to die to my lust. But I do—upward to Him. And moments later there is complete freedom from that tyranny of the "drink denied." I have been loosed from my lust. I can breathe again. And in place of that hunger which only wants more, I am satisfied...Victory over my sin—His victory—has given me an increment of life. Himself. I've made the real Connection. He is my sin-bearer, my sin-taker, my Resurrection, and my Life!" (Impossible Joy by Ron J. p. 15)

The surrender to our lust-bearer in the heat of the moment is Jesus's great provision before the Father. It is why he stands before the Father eternally, day and night, as our intercessor in our time of need. Jesus has entered heaven itself on our behalf. He is available to us in every moment of weakness, fear and trouble. But according to Hebrews, it is up to us to choose to draw near and avail ourselves of his merciful presence and provision for lust.

Eight

ONCE FOR ALL: FINDING THE CONNECTION
THAT SAVES FROM LUST

*What is My Life Without Your Love? Tell
me who am I without you by my side?*

GEORGE HARRISON

*You love me
You complete me
You hold my heart in your hands
And it's okay cause I trust that
You'll be the best man that you can.*

KEISHA COLE

What is the connection that saves from lust? It is the immediate, intimate, personal encounter with Jesus at the moment of our temptation. To make this saving connection, we must believe that Jesus wants to connect with us in our weakness. Too many Christians motivated by shame or control attempt to withdraw from God in their moments of lust. I can remember a spiritual yet almost tangible turning away from God in my moments of acting out. I would attempt to remove myself from God, as if I was engaging in a private activity apart from his presence. But rather than attempt to hide our difficulty or attempt to handle it on our own, in order to be free, we must believe that Jesus wants to move toward our lust, so he can lovingly bear it for us. This very act of Jesus moving toward our lust allows us to move away from our lust by simply giving it to him. For all lust addicts, we must meet him here or we do not meet him at all.

The problem with many of us is that we too easily are drawn to other potential connections that offer to fill the hole in our soul. One of these is the romantic or sexual connection. There are vast quantities of cultural messages designed to support this false hope of deliverance.

Many popular songs proclaim the power and satisfaction of finding one's "soul mate." Songs like those above extol the blessings in being "completed" by love or the lost feeling of living "without your love." But behind these feelings lurks possible and even likely dependency, the idea that someone else will make up what is lacking in me. Sometimes, this is called "love addiction" or "desperate attachment." Its severest forms can lead to a kind of possessive and controlling violence and even murder when the object of this attachment chooses to walk out of the desperate person's life. Christopher West elaborates on a much needed corrective.

"It is entirely human to yearn for marital love. Yet we must be careful never to 'hang our hats on a hook that cannot bear the weight.' Anyone who looks to marriage as his ultimate fulfillment is setting himself up for serious disillusionment. Realizing that earthly marriage is only a sign of the heavenly marriage to come and that the union to come (with the heavenly bridegroom) is a gift extended to everyone without exception, takes a tremendous burden off people's expectations for ultimate happiness through marriage in this life…As a married man, I am first to extol the joys of married life. But these are only a foretaste, only a foreshadowing of the eternal joys to come."(Theology of the Body Explained, p. 325-6).

Author and Speaker Vicki Tiede has said "The best gift a woman can give to her husband is to love God more than him." The irony is that loving God above all human relationships frees us to give the healthiest kind of love to our spouse, children, family and friends.

While some people attempt to find their ultimate connection in romantic connections or married love, others will seek to sooth their soul through religion and ritual.

In Hebrews 9, we arrive at the heart of the powerlessness to which "religion" alone is confined. The author now demonstrates his familiarity with the Jewish sacrifices in great detail, their origin, their order and significance. He knows where every piece of furniture and every article is positioned in the "earthly tent." Hebrews 9:1-5 speaks of the lampstand, table and bread of the presence, the second curtain, the Most Holy Place and so on.

Now even the first covenant had regulations for worship and an earthly place of holiness. 2 For a tent[a] was prepared, the first section, in which were the lampstand and the table and the bread of the Presence.[b] It is called the Holy Place. 3 Behind the second curtain was a second section[c] called the Most Holy Place, 4 having the golden altar of incense and the ark of the covenant covered on all sides with gold, in which was a golden urn holding the manna, and Aaron's staff that budded, and the tablets of the covenant. 5 Above it were the cherubim of glory overshadowing the mercy seat. Of these things we cannot now speak in detail. (Hebrews 9:1-5)

First century Jewish readers would no doubt be familiar with every article in the tabernacle. However, the writer's stark and sweeping conclusion is without qualification: He points them away from their former experience of these things to the eternal and substantial realities to which they point. The actual objects, are, in fact, mere shadows, images that point to authentic, unchangeable realities.

"According to this arrangement, gifts and sacrifices are offered that cannot perfect the conscience of the worshipper, but deal only with food and drink and various washings, regulations for the body imposed until the time of reformation." (Hebrews 9:9b-10.) This scene in the "earthly place of holiness" (Verse 1) is pointing to something higher and better, to the coming of something else which will eclipse the ritualistic practice of the earthly tent and present humanity with an altogether different way to connect with God, a reality to which these objects point.

But how do we interpret this in the context of our theme of freedom from lust? All of us who struggle with the wash, rinse and repeat cycle of sin are caught in a cycle of ritual. Just as the writer of Hebrews is speaking about a religious ritual from which believers in Jesus have been set free, so lust drunks are also caught in a ritual which bears certain characteristics.

Every addict engages in a ritual, one that leads us to "the point of no return." It is the experiential place after which we know we are going to act out. We have crossed the Rubicon. There is no turning back. Our ritual may involve a certain night of the week, or when our spouse leaves town for a trip, or attending parties with alcohol or simply logging onto our computer in a certain frame of mind or at a certain time of night. It might involve a trip to the ATM machine or a drive to a certain part of town or an encounter with a certain kind of person.

Some of these rituals will bear enough similarity to a real relationship or marital connection to the opposite sex that we will practice them for years believing that they are a "preview of coming attractions." Lust often masquerades itself as a "waiting room for marriage." But as discussed previously, it is not. Much like the temple ritual, many lust addicts will fill the gap with their ritual until "it no longer works for me." The message of Hebrews is that the temple worship was never meant to "work for us." Instead, it was meant to point us to something better, more enduring, eternal.

Those who act out sexually are quite familiar with this phenomenon. Our ritualistic practice has driven us away from human community, intimacy and honesty, just as Gollum was driven away into the Misty Mountains to the dark and dank places of isolation. Our ritual demonstrates our powerlessness over and over again and we cannot recover and achieve any long-term sobriety unless and until we acknowledge the specific and repetitive nature of this powerlessness in Step 1. Our ritual has us caught in a snare, one from which we cannot remove ourselves.

However, before we are able to admit complete powerlessness, what Frederick Buechner called the "magnificent defeat" that enables all future victories, most of us will end up being caught in this repeat cycle for years, trying to relieve ourselves from fear, isolation, loneliness, anger and depression by acting out. But what we discover is that this temporary relief our addiction offers simply drives us deeper into it. The inevitable consequences it generates are testimonies to its fruit, dishonesty, despair, a loss of intimacy, financial distress, employment problems, disease, jail time and even potential death. I am always amazed at the number of people in lust recovery who have said in so many words, "This addiction almost killed me."

Religious ritual, while less overtly troubling, also drives us into despair as well. How many church attendees find themselves wrapped around the axle of anguished living year after year, looking for some kind of breakthrough? How many run from church to church, seminar to seminar, book to book or evangelist to evangelist seeking "the answer?" The reason so many television evangelists preach about "breakthroughs" is because so many of us are looking for them, perhaps wanting to find an instant cure to long-standing issues. This syndrome of "running through the thistles," finding transformation without pain or the passage of time, as attractive as it may be, is rarely the way we find change. In the midst of this search, we often keep our religious rituals because, not only because they offer some kind of discipline, but because they are so familiar and we have little idea what else we should do.

So what do the religious and the lust ritual have in common? Two things.

First, religious and lust rituals are driven by human effort. Many a person who struggles with lust has been told to "read your Bible and pray more." But what are strugglers to do when they make a serious and sustained effort with no result? The Apostle Paul certainly possessed the most pristine religious resume of his day. He outlined it in Philippians 3. "If anyone else thinks he has reason for confidence in the flesh, I have more: 5 circumcised on the eighth day, of the people of Israel, of the tribe of

Benjamin, a Hebrew of Hebrews; as to the law, a Pharisee; [6] as to zeal, a persecutor of the church; as to righteousness under the law, [c]blameless." (Philippians 3:4-6)

Yet it all ended in serious character defects, persecution of innocent people and complicity in murder. In first century days, there was no more serious and sustained effort than temple worship and sacrifice. When it failed and the temple was destroyed, the entire enterprise had to be re-examined. What in the world was God doing? Hebrews explains that the whole sacrificial system, though instituted by God through Moses was only temporary. It pointed to a more permanent solution. What was that solution? "...he (Christ) entered once for all into the holy places, not by means of the blood of goats and calves but by means of his own blood, thus securing an eternal redemption." (Hebrews 9:12.) An "eternal redemption" is never repeated. It is permanent. Religious ritual can be healthy as a way of living out one's discipleship, but it is a poor transformational fix for deep-seated issues like sex addiction. In 12 Step terms, until one has worked the deeply spiritual steps One through Three, it is too early to "do the work" of Steps Four through Nine. In fact, if the surrender in Step 3 has not taken place, Steps 4-9 will not work.

When we are practicing sex addicts engaged in our ritual, we are continually "paying the price" for our addiction. Family members also suffer, as will as others close to us. The ritual of lusting and acting out is a ritual of self-abuse with radiated pain to ourselves and others. We have been people who have asked God to take away our addiction, but we have also doubted that he would, not understanding that "...the one who doubts is like a wave of the sea that is driven and tossed by the wind." (James 1:6) This is why Step 2 is so crucial, allowing to God enter the picture and coming to believe a power greater than ourselves can restore us to sanity. "And without faith it is impossible to please him...," (Hebrews 11:6a) let alone "draw near."

Secondly, both religious and lust rituals cannot purify the conscience. This may seem obvious but not to the lust addict. In a tragic way the lust addict acts out because this is the only way he or she knows to "get rid of it." Many of us have "white knuckled" through a day or a weekend trying not to act out and only ending up yielding so we can just "get it over with." We don't know surrender because we have never been able to live a lifestyle of surrender, to make habitual surrender in the heat of the moment part of our way of life. We do not understand that all feelings can be surrendered. I remember the day in recovery when I realized I never had to act out again if I was simply willing to surrender the specific feeling of the moment. I might have to make a phone call to a recovery brother, but I had to understand that feelings alone do not compel us to act out. But to whom do we surrender? Our problem is one of connection, but we need someone to connect to. What are we to do?

Man has attempted to purify his conscience from time immemorial by appeasing gods and ritual sacrifice. Many of these attempts ended by visiting temple prostitutes, a practice universal in the ancient world. But the Christian gospel brought something the world had never seen before, the message, power and connection that made all the difference, what Bill W called 'the expulsive power of a new affection," an intimate connection with God. This is what the tabernacle furniture points to, especially the Bread of the Presence. Jesus is the one we can truly feed on, the bread of life who satisfies our hunger, available 24/7 to us who believe. "I am the living bread that came down from heaven. If anyone eats of this bread, he will live forever." (John 6:51)

When Jesus met the Woman of Samaria in John 4, she was caught up in two rituals, her sexual ritual and her working ritual. Her sexual ritual was revealed in the five men she had been married to and the unmarried relationship in which she currently lived. Her drawing water in the heat of the day, likely to avoid the wagging tongues of the more respectable females in town, characterized the repetitive nature of her life. Her two rituals are expressed in one comment to Jesus. "Sir, give me this water so that I will not be thirsty or have to come here to draw water." (John 4:15) We can sense the utter weariness in her words.

But Jesus had previously given her a promise, a lifestyle exit ramp. "Everyone who drinks of this water will be thirsty again but whoever drinks of the water that I will give him will never be thirsty again." (John 4:14) There is only one true reality that can satisfy those of us who believe, Jesus's eternal and available presence. This is the water of salvation, his thirst-quenching presence. As Isaiah said, "With joy you will draw water from the wells of salvation. And you will say in that day: Give thanks to the Lord, call upon his name, make known his deeds among the peoples, proclaim that his name is exalted." (Isaiah 12:3-4)

Thirdly, Jesus sacrifice once for all on the cross has ended our dependency on religious and sexual rituals and opened the way to God at every moment of our lives. "For Christ has entered not into holy places made with hands, which are copies of true things, but into heaven itself, now to appear in heaven on our behalf." (Hebrews 9:24)

In Hebrews, there is one characteristic of rituals that drives home this powerlessness, the inability to "perfect the conscience." It is a fact that temples "made with hands" cannot deliver us. Because temples cannot save us, Jesus had to enter "heaven itself?" Why? To appear there on our behalf as our mediator, bearing his own shed blood, to both make atonement and to intercede for us. The real holy place is not on earth, made by human hands, but in heaven itself.

It is remarkable that a Jew like the Apostle Paul could say the following words while preaching at Athens. "The God who made the world and everything in it, being Lord of heaven and earth, does not live in temples made by man, nor is he served by human hands, as though he needed anything, since he himself gives to us life and breath and everything." How could a Jew say this? Paul's direct audience were Greeks who littered their surroundings with pagan temples. (Including the one in Corinth inhabited by more than a thousand temple prostitutes.) But the same could have been said of the Temple in Jerusalem and its human propelled sacrificial system! It had become for many an end in itself and a dead one at that. The message of Hebrews is that Christ's once for all sacrifice of himself sets us free from ritualistic works, either religious or sexual, so we can serve 'the living God."

"For if the blood of goats and bulls, and the sprinkling of defiled persons with the ashes of a heifer, sanctify[f] for the purification of the flesh, [14] how much more will the blood of Christ, who through the eternal Spirit offered himself without blemish to God, purify our[g]conscience from dead works to serve the living God.' (Hebrews 9:13-14)

A Final Exhortation: Sobriety or Judgment

The once for all nature of Christ's sacrifice, one that makes intimacy with God truly possible comes with a warning, one that is tied up with our free will and the unchangeable link between actions and consequences.

Many Christians are confused on this point. They mistakenly believe that God's forgiveness somehow insulates us from consequences. It does not. Many a sex addict has discovered that when he or she stops acting out, weeks, months and years must pass before negative consequences start to abate. A spouse may remain angry for some time, children alienated or the addict himself or herself may remain unemployed or in jail. It is only over time that things begin to change for the positive and then only as the addict stays sober and works their program.

Before I surrendered my addiction, I watched a video produced by a Christian therapist. She spoke of the "sin unto death" and outlined the following scenario, one that made me shudder and contributed to my letting go months later. She said that although God will restore us at any time, when we become mired in our addiction, we will often disbelieve that He can. Perhaps we believe that we have "gone too far," or are "beyond hope." We are so caught up in addiction that we give up on ourselves, perhaps even imagining that God has given up on us, even though he has not. What I and others have learned about "surrender" is that God will not override our wills. He will not do for us what only we can do, namely desire Him above our addiction. Perhaps it is why God often uses the binge to drive home the reality of powerlessness so that in despairing of our own devices, we finally surrender to Him. We often have to get worse before we get better. Do we become afraid when a fellow addict goes on a binge? It may be that a binge is necessary before the choice becomes in their own mind, "find God or die."

In his second epistle, Peter speaks of this state of being hopelessly caught up in addiction. Notice he is speaking to believers here, not to those who have never known Christ.

[18] For, speaking loud boasts of folly, they entice by sensual passions of the flesh those who are barely escaping from those who live in error. [19] They promise them freedom, but they themselves are slaves[a] of corruption. For whatever overcomes a person, to that he is enslaved. [20] For if, after they have escaped the defilements of the world through the knowledge of our Lord and Savior Jesus Christ, they are again entangled in them and overcome, the last state has become worse for them than the first. [21] For it would have been better for them never to have known the way of righteousness than after knowing it to turn back from the holy commandment delivered to them. [22] What the true proverb says has happened to them: "The dog returns to its own vomit, and the sow, after washing herself, returns to wallow in the mire." (2 Peter 2:18-22)

Apparently, the wash, rinse repeat cycle is not a modern invention. What we become "entangled in" (verse 20) defines our consequences. Peter is describing believers who can be corrupted by people and circumstances that involve "sensual passions of the flesh." These seducers may have been Gnostics who taught a kind of non-connection between body and spirit, releasing people by their teaching to indulge in lust. They were apparently quite successful with those who were "barely escaping" that lifestyle. Interestingly, studies have shown that addicted people who are sober for a time and then return to it manifest similar decline as if they had never left their addicted lifestyle. Sometimes those who have been sober years on end and then succumb can find it difficult to find their way back to recovery. These are consequences we must understand lest we fall back into old habits. Those who are sober always contain within themselves the possibility of slipping or relapsing. That is why the real key to recovery is never only the surrender of the addiction, but learning to live dependently on Jesus. The person who says in his heart, "I'm fixed. No more problems," is likely to return to his or her folly because the character defect of ego, pride or isolation was what got them into lust addiction to begin with.

But the once for all nature of Christ's sacrifice leads to another implication. For just as Christ ended the estrangement between God and man, there will be a time for judgment ahead. Life on earth runs out. How we finish is all important.

"And I heard a voice from heaven saying, "Write this: Blessed are the dead who die in the Lord from now on." "Blessed indeed," says the Spirit, "that they may rest from their labors, for their deeds follow them!" (Revelation 14:13.)

The judgment of our deeds is not to be confused with salvation by grace. The writer of Hebrews makes the distinction clear.

"But as it is, he has appeared once for all at the end of the ages to put away sin by the sacrifice of himself. [27] And just as it is appointed for man to die once, and after that comes judgment, [28] so Christ, having been offered once to bear the sins of many, will appear a second time, not to deal with sin but to save those who are eagerly waiting for him." Hebrews 9:27-28

This has both psychological and spiritual implications for those struggling with lust. Part of the psychology of sexual addiction is the illusion that life can continually be "new." The porn addict searches for the new image, situation, race or sexual practice. The serial adulterer believes the next relationship will be the one that fixes him or her. For the lust addict life becomes a prison of possibilities, never settling down to invest for the long term. Juggling relationships and intermittent internet porn use mask the reality that our life clocks are ticking down. Life running out seems cruel to a mirage of endless possibilities. Denying our mortality makes us lose touch with the necessary reality of making the right choices.

And so the addict creates the illusion that we can restart our lives and constantly begin again. But the reality is we are spending life. We are aging. We are only allowed a certain amount of time on this earth. Sumner Redstone, who holds controlling interests in both CBS and Viacom, was quoted in the Vanity Fair (The May 31st 2015 Issue). "I will not discuss succession. You know why? I'm not going to die." But he will die. We all do. The question becomes, in what state will our inevitable death occur. And what will be our legacy?

Do you remember the famous line from the soap opera, Days of Our Lives? "As sands through the hourglass, so are the days of our lives." The same sentiment is expressed more profoundly in Psalm 90. Notice the reference to "secret sins," the ultimate losing bet in the attempt to cheat father time.

> You return man to dust
>   and say, "Return, O children of man!"[b]
> [4] For a thousand years in your sight
>   are but as yesterday when it is past,
>   or as a watch in the night.
> [5] You sweep them away as with a flood; they are like a dream,
>   like grass that is renewed in the morning:
> [6] in the morning it flourishes and is renewed;
>   in the evening it fades and withers.
> [7] For we are brought to an end by your anger;
>   by your wrath we are dismayed.
> [8] You have set our iniquities before you,
>   our secret sins in the light of your presence.
> [9] For all our days pass away under your wrath;
>   we bring our years to an end like a sigh.
> [10] The years of our life are seventy,
>   or even by reason of strength eighty;
> yet their span[c] is but toil and trouble;
>   they are soon gone, and we fly away.

The spiritual significance of the coming judgment of our works is that some works are not significant. They are "wood, hay and stubble."

"Now if anyone builds on the foundation with gold, silver, precious stones, wood, hay, straw— [13] each one's work will become manifest, for the Day will disclose it, because it will be revealed by fire, and the fire will test what sort of work each one has done." (I Corinthians 3:12-13.) Some things we do in this life do not last. Apparently, despite our chasing them, they did not ultimately matter. Others possess deep and lasting significance. But what about evil deeds, wounds caused to others and ourselves?

When I got sober, I began to contemplate my legacy. I was 59 years old and my father had died the previous year, allowing me to take my place as next in the male in line on our family tree. There was no avoiding this stark reality. In the moment of turning, a voice spoke to me saying. "You have promised to surrender this addiction when you turned 20, 30, 40 and 50 and it hasn't worked. You are about to turn 60. Who is kidding whom?" Time was running out. I was going to leave a legacy. The only question was: What kind would it be?

I believe mercy is often hidden in judgment. The "sands in the hourglass" were now not my enemy but my friend, causing me to focus on how I would spend whatever years I had left. "Clearing away the wreckage of my past," I began to focus on helping others, spending time with my family, writing down what God had shown me and being a good steward of my remaining years, fulfilling the Biblical admonition of "making the best use of the time, because the days are evil. (Ephesians 5:16.) We will return to the themes of legacy and destiny later on as we contemplate "the city not made with hands."

Nine

THE NEW AND LIVING WAY: HAVING
FAITH AND PRESERVING OUR SOULS

"The flesh is the hinge of salvation."

TERTULLIAN

10 For since the law has but a shadow of the good things to come instead of the true form of these realities, it can never, by the same sacrifices that are continually offered every year, make perfect those who draw near. ² Otherwise, would they not have ceased to be offered, since the worshipers, having once been cleansed, would no longer have any consciousness of sins? ³ But in these sacrifices there is a reminder of sins every year. ⁴ For it is impossible for the blood of bulls and goats to take away sins.

⁵ Consequently, when Christ[a] came into the world, he said,

"Sacrifices and offerings you have not desired,
　　but a body have you prepared for me;
⁶ in burnt offerings and sin offerings
　　you have taken no pleasure.
⁷ Then I said, 'Behold, I have come to do your will, O God,
　　as it is written of me in the scroll of the book.'" (Hebrews 10:1-7)

"This life's dim windows of the soul
Distorts the heavens from pole to pole
And leads you to believe a lie
When you see with, not through, the eye." William Blake

The above quote from the romantic poet William Blake demonstrates how easy it is for us humans to focus on "the law (which) has but a shadow of the good things to come" rather than on "the true form of these realities." (Hebrews 10:1.) Like these Hebrew Christians, we can see physical objects (shadows) right in front of us and at the same time miss the substance to which they point. According to Hebrews, when we are bound by an earthly, overly particularized or shadowy vision, we miss the heavenly substantial one.

These Jewish believers were tempted to focus on the machinations of temple worship, a center of religious life and activity that after AD 70 was completely destroyed. It has never been rebuilt. This spiritual state bound them to an unchangeable past. Because they were preoccupied in looking back to what was gone, they were in danger of missing what God had provided for them in Jesus. Standing in the shadow of temple-centered sacrifice, these Jewish believers were in danger of missing the eternal provision purchased at the cost of Jesus' own blood.

The only way Hebrew believers could embrace the gospel fully was if they could somehow understand that temple worship was destined by God himself to cease because it pointed to something greater which was yet to come. Therefore, the writer challenges them to be like the acrobat, who must let go of one trapeze in order to grasp the other. Letting go, catching and re-gripping requires faith. This is why he writes that God "does away with the first in order to establish the second." (Verse 9.) The sacrifices of temple worship discussed in Hebrews 10 and previously cannot deliver true intimacy with God and therefore quench the fires of lust and other sins because of their man-centered and repetitive nature. Temple priests repeatedly offering animal sacrifices cannot take away sin. (Verse 1.)

In fact, this is what we lust addicts have attempted to do through our addiction rituals performed on a regular basis. The lust addict believes a similar thing to Jewish believers looking back to physical yet shadowy realities. We have looked to objectified human bodies or least an objectified human image to get through life. This is our ritual dependence, which derives every bit as much from bondage as the ritual sacrifice of the ancient world. I once heard a women say "Give me a priest." It was as if she was saying "I need a flesh and blood mediator to get me through the day or the week." But the Scriptures tell us "...there is one God, and there is one mediator between God and men, the man Christ Jesus, (I Timothy 2:5) Neither religious nor sexual ritual can satisfy the human heart because they are based on what we attempt to do for ourselves rather than allowing Jesus to accomplish it on our behalf. To allow him to do what he is uniquely qualified to do, we must not only let go of our ritual, we must humble ourselves before him daily and ask for his immediate presence and provision for lust.

To understand the universal nature of addictive ritual, we must understand that it was as universal in the pagan world as in the Jewish world. When the Christian gospel came to Ephesus, the message presented an imminent threat to the Temple of Artemis (Roman: Diana). Her name means "great or holy." She was the goddess of the hunt, an appropriate symbol for those who are continually chasing lust. Fittingly, she is depicted covered with breasts. (See photo below)

The image of a human, man or woman, who can provide everything we are looking for is as old as time and plays a central role in humanity's on-going choices between idolatry and the worship of the one true God. One of lust's demands in the human heart is the insistent voice of "must have." A husband or wife who "must have" sexual relations with their spouse is under the sway of lust. How many times have you heard a close Christian friend confide in you, "I have to have sex at least once a ____ or I get antsy." Only when sex becomes truly optional, whether single or married, do we become free to worship the one true God who "gave us life and breath and everything." (Acts 17:28)

Part of the struggle is not simply to surrender lust but to actually be free enough to affirm another's dignity, worth and even beauty. God's plan is to not only free us from lust but to engage with the opposite sex in healthy, life-affirming ways. Christopher West explains that, "men have their own a priori responsibility to...assert every woman's true value and dignity." He tells the story of a woman who attended "a Catholic college where students genuinely desire to grow in holiness. She shared with me the emotional effects of having men for three years continually turn away or look at the sidewalk whenever she walked across campus. Those men may have needed to do this in order to avoid lusting. But was there not one man on that campus pure enough to look at her and in so doing affirm her dignity rather than lust after her?" (TOB Explained, page 235) How can we become people who not only surrender lust but can affirm the full presence of others? This must begin with our relationship with the God who fills the hungry and thirsty soul often diverted to lust.

The God of the Jews and Christians offered an alternative to the pagan provision of idolatry and sexual lust. Harriet Lutzky, who is the adjunct assistant professor of psychology at John Jay College, City University of New York, has presented evidence that Shaddai was an attribute of a Semitic goddess, linking the epithet Shaddai with the Hebrew *šad* meaning "breast", giving the meaning "the one of the breast.." (Wikipedia).

The astonishing claim is that the sexual lust that so often drives us and we think of as a legitimate need may in many cases be a short-circuiting of a deeper and spiritual connection with God, one that our deepest heart longs for, one that leaves no residue of shame or regret. What an

inspiration it has also been to me to see men previous troubled by lust actually become able to affirm and engage with women without resorting to
their prior state. He is truly the God who restores.

When Jesus asks his followers to eat and drink of his "body and blood,"
can there be any clearer invitation that feeding on him is the real answer
to the hunger and thirst of our sexual longings? A prayer of the lust addict often goes like this. "I pray, Lord, that I will find in you what my lust
is really looking for." Only when we find in God what our lust is looking
for will we stop putting god-like pressure on other humans to satisfy our
misplaced God hunger.

This is not to denigrate sex in any way. Sex is a God-given blessing
and provision, one invented by God himself for a whole variety of reasons,
including procreation, self-giving, a sign of the binding of two people together in marriage, and a picture of the ultimate "spousal union" with
Christ in heaven. But no marriage can slake the thirst of lust, nor exhaust
it so that lust never threatens that marriage. It was never designed to do
that. As John Paul II points out in Theology of the Body, marriage was created by God at the time of man's innocence to be an outlet for self-giving,
not for taking, objectifying or lusting. No, God himself, is the provision
for our lust because He provides what lust can never provide, the eternal
connection, the presence we are all looking for, the union and feast we are
both invited to and destined for.

So we might ask ourselves, "What does pagan lust have to do with
Christianity, the religion of the one true God?" Paganism is an easy target
because of its blatant idolatry. It certainly has and will continue to expose
human drives and their misappropriation. Its re-emergence in our day is
both aggressive and predictable, particularly as Christianity is demonized
in the popular press, Hollywood and academia. But the writer of Hebrews
indicates that focusing on the ritual performance of Jewish sacrifices can be
equally a dead end. He presents a variety of reasons in chapter 10. Among
these are that these sacrifices are repetitive, reinforcing the notion that human problems that cannot be truly solved by them. (Verses 1b-3.) Washing
clothes in your home washing machine might get the dirt out, but it does

nothing to prevent the same clothes from getting dirty again. Secondly, these are merely animal sacrifices, which cannot "take away sin." v. 4. Animals are not humans and bear little resemblance to the offenses of those humans. In other words, they are a ritual without a permanent solution, focused on the wrong kind of sacrifice, making them doubly powerless over human sin.

We have spoken about the lust addict subjected to a ritual without result, the cyclical problem of temptation, short-term euphoria, withdrawal, and back to temptation. What might this ritual look like?

The addict logs onto the internet or travels to the ATM machine or to a certain segment of town. He or she visits Facebook or a favorite rendezvous internet site, and then proceeds to act out sexually, usually in ways he or she has done many times before. But engaging in the ritual does not rid us of it. Try as we might, we were people of the "temporary fix." Often possessed by these feelings, we were people wanting to "get it over with" and get back to our day. Many addicts tell us that even in the middle of acting out, they are actually planning the rest of their day as if they have to "take care of business" in order to be freed from the addictive cycle. The ancient world was filled with such sentiments. Many people would visit a pagan shrine to worship and visit the temple prostitute next door either before or after. God himself understood the cyclical nature of this ritual and its futility.

⁶ The LORD said to me in the days of King Josiah: "Have you seen what she did, that faithless one, Israel, how she went up on every high hill and under every green tree, and there played the whore? ⁷ And I thought, 'After she has done all this she will return to me,' but she did not return,… (Jeremiah 3:6-7b)

Many commentators and preachers have spiritualized passages like these. But what we should see is the spiritual nature of sexual sin, as well as the sexualized nature of spiritual sin. This is why lust and character defects are always together in an unbreakable link.

Many lust addicts, having acted out with porn or a person, have told themselves, "Well, I won't have to do that again for a while, maybe ever!" But we were wrong. Resolutions without inner transformation availed us nothing. What was actually happening was that we were reinforcing the behavior, virtually assuring that we would return to it again and again. Like Abraham's "ram caught in a thicket" we were the sacrifice, bound to our fate. Just as it is "impossible for the blood of bulls and goats to take away sin," v. 4, so our own sexualized rituals will never take away our addictive behavior.

There is only one who can and he has come to inhabit our human struggle, to meet us there in the fullness of our fallen nature. His purpose is to spin us out of our ritual once and for all, to nullify the gravitational pull of our lust. He does it by entering our very struggle, identifying with every pull of our weakened humanity, dying on the cross, rising to new life and interceding before the Father for us now moment by moment. He asks us to invite him into our struggle.

"Sacrifices and burnt offerings you have not desired, but a body you have prepared for me; in burnt offerings and sin offerings you have taken no pleasure. Then I said, "behold I have come to do your will, O God, as it is written of me in the scroll of the book." (Hebrews 10:5b-7)

Why did he Jesus do it? One reason was to shock us out of our shame and unbelief, to deliver us from the double-bind of law and shame. Christopher West, in Theology of the Body Explained puts it this way.

"You don't believe in the Father's love? Let me make it real for you; let me incarnate it for you so that you can taste and see. You don't believe that God wants to give you life? I will bleed myself dry so that my blood can vivify you. You thought God was a tyrant, a slave driver? You thought he would whip your back if you gave him a chance? I will take the form of a slave; I will let you whip my back and nail me to a tree; I will let you lord it over me to show you that the Father has no desire to lord it over you. I have not come to condemn you, but to save you. I have not come to enslave you, but to set you free. Turn from your disbelief. Believe and receive the gift of eternal life I offer you."

Only in his sacrifice, once for all, can our lust ritual possibly end. Why? Because our ritual was bound to repetition and never-ending performance, to moral energy and effort, which in the end always fail us. Jews had to return to the temple every year. Priests had to offer repeated sacrifices "that could never take away sin." And we are bound to our ritual until we are see the way out God has provided in Jesus and allow him to take us there.

One of the conundrums in the recovering community is why it takes so long for some people to become sober and why some never become sober. The temptation is to come up with some kind of formula, psychological reasoning or childhood block that once removed will set us free. We are tempted to believe that our ritual or knowledge or some power we possess can fix us. We see others "working the program" and staying sober. Why can't we? But that is not the solution. A wise sponsor was once asked by a constantly slipping sponsee, "Why can't I stay sober?" His answer was. "That's not up to you. Your responsibility is to work your program." But can the program, the 12 Steps make us sober? No, not even the program can do that for us. The universal testimony is that only God himself, only an "authentic spiritual experience" of him can do this. The reason our wise sponsor encouraged the slipping sponsee to "work the program" is that this is likely the best chance our friend will have to be close enough to God to let go. Our sobriety rests with God and he is the one who keeps us sober. Some people have "high bottoms." Others must end up in the physical or spiritual gutter. Only God knows why. We only know that everyone must let go to be sober. There seems to be something indispensible about the human will in relationship to God that even God himself will not violate. He appears to want a relationship with us that requires our wanting it too. Lust addiction occupies the very same space in us that God wants to inhabit. Until we surrender lust, he cannot occupy it.

This is why preaching aimed at "moral reform" will never work. As a lust addict, I was never going to surrender in response to moralism or trying harder as an incentive to sobriety. (It isn't one.) An addict encouraged to "read your Bible and pray more" will often perceive this as an exercise in despair because his view of God as disapproving makes him want to run the other way. In Matthew 25, the man with one talent hid it in the ground because he was 'afraid." He just knew (however wrongly) who the master was. "Master, I knew you to be a hard man, reaping where you did not sow, and gathering where you scattered no seed..." (Matthew 25:24) But was this the master's true nature? Or was this the distortion of a mind gripped in paralyzing fear unable to let go and trust?

Only after I see the love and kindness of God's gift and surrender in response to him, can effort do anything for me. Once sobriety comes, there will be lots of things to do, and effort exerted, but "doing things" will never get us sober. Jesus's own coming in the flesh and bearing the full consequences of our lust gives us a shot, because his bearing our lust allows us to give up our ritual. It gives us a chance at sobriety and recovery because we see, perhaps for the first time, the futile corruption of our human will. This is the spiritual necessity created in the first three Steps of AA. The alcoholic (or sexaholic in this case) has seen that he or she is utterly unable to quit on their own and stay quit. (Step 1) Progress by human will and effort must be surrendered as hopeless before the possibility of divine help can enter as remedy. (Step 2) The option of surrender then becomes both real and necessary. (Step 3)

The old phrase in the Anglican 39 Articles was "very far gone from original righteousness." But the discerning eye of the recovering community and the addict themselves can see emerging hope in this powerlessness. In fact, to work a real 12 Step program, one's powerlessness must be documented as a matter of record in Step 1. If there is any question about this, perhaps the addict needs another binge or to venture out "to do more research." Only then can we come to a place of believing that God could restore us to sanity. Only then does the addict in Step 3 "turn our will and our lives over to the care of God as we understood God."

We in the church often speak of the "finished work of Christ." Hebrews gives us a visual image of this in Chapter 1 when the writer says, "After making purification for sins, he sat down at the right hand of the majesty on high." (Hebrews 1:3b) Jesus sitting down means his work is complete, never to be repeated for all the reasons we have discussed. In Chapter 10, the result of this work is revealed. "I will remember their sins and their lawless deeds no more." (10:17) This is a quote from Jeremiah 31, a purple passage from the Old Testament quoted in Hebrews 8:8-12 and now reiterated in part in Chapter 10. This finished work is the sole basis for deep spiritual rest for all addicts and sinners and the theme of this book.

Essential understanding for us is that attempting to "pay for" our sins is part of our human problem. Sin and toil have been inextricably linked since Genesis 3. After the fall, God said to Adam,

> By the sweat of your face
> > you shall eat bread,
> till you return to the ground,
> > for out of it you were taken;
> for you are dust,
> > and to dust you shall return." (Genesis 3:19)

Because of this intimate connection between toil and sin, lust and other addictions often exhaust us. It is as if we have been condemned to our addiction in similar fashion to our work. And so we hear stories of alcoholics lying in the street exhausted or porn addicts watching porn all night into the wee hours of the morning. Many lose all track of time and simply dress for work without any sleep, beginning another day in an exhausted state.

> The iniquities of the wicked ensnare him,
> > and he is caught in the toils of his sin.
> 23 He dies for lack of discipline,
> > and because of his great folly he is lost. (Proverbs 5:22-23 RSV)

What is the point? It is simply that performance driven religion and the lust binge contain more similarities than we might acknowledge. Both are attempts to purge ourselves of troubling feelings and neither is ever successful in doing so. However, often they do work as truth tellers about the futility of toil and the despair of "dead works." But there is a remedy.

How much more, then, will the blood of Christ, who through the eternal Spirit offered himself unblemished to God, cleanse our consciences from acts that lead to death, so that we may serve the living God! (Hebrews 9:14.)

Ultimately, only resting in the finished work of Christ can bring our own rest. Feeding on his sufficiency, not our own, will work, because He is both what our lust is really looking for and the answer to our never-ending lust ritual.

Ten

THE LUST ADDICT FACES DEATH

14 Since therefore the children share in flesh and blood,
he himself likewise partook of the same things, that
through death he might destroy the one who has the power
of death, that is, the devil, 15 and deliver all those who
through fear of death were subject to lifelong slavery.

(HEBREWS 2:14-15)

"He loved and hated it as he loved and hated himself."

JRR TOLKIEN ON GOLLUM AND THE RING

One of my favorite New Testament passages occurs at the end of John's gospel when Jesus restores Peter. The words Jesus says to him have provoked much reflection throughout my life. "Truly, truly I say to you, when you were young, you used to dress yourself and walk where you wanted, but when you are old, you will stretch out your hands, and another will dress you and carry you where you do not want to go." (John 21:18). These are challenging words to 21st century Christians because we preach a gospel that majors in the idea of "freedom." But we distort the meaning of the word by confining its meaning to free choice and a truncated notion of an adventurous kind of living. We confuse the biblical understanding of freedom by what we omit. Having our hands bound and being led away doesn't fit into a globe-trotting, "world is your oyster" lifestyle. Perhaps we have adopted an American view or a pagan view of freedom rather than the gospel view. In any case, here Jesus brings Peter back to confront his biggest fear, that of losing personal autonomy. Wasn't this why Peter opted out of Jesus's mission in the first place and ended up denying him despite Peter's protestations of courage?

Peter had heard Jesus teaching about the unity between disciple and master, between the one who sends and the one who is sent. He knew that Jesus's destiny contained hints of his own. He was afraid and denied his Lord.

After repeating Peter's initial call by the lake in John 21, and asking him once again to "Follow me," Jesus tells Peter that he will be bound by others and led away. We do not know whether Peter continued to wrestle with his destiny or not. But we do know he eventually embraced it. In the movie Quo Vadis (Where Are You Going?), Peter is tempted to leave Rome under persecution. Instead, he turns around and embraces both his ministry and his call to suffering.

This idea that we are bound to Jesus, come what may, is a challenging but necessary calling for us as believers. When Dietrich Bonhoeffer left Nazi Germany to come to America in the late 1930's, he subsequently became troubled by his continued absence from his native land. Though he appreciated what America had to offer, he knew that he must return to Germany because his country and the German church needed him. Despite the danger, Bonhoeffer chose the dangerous and unsafe path because he was called to it. Likewise, until we learn to move forward despite our fears, and go where Jesus calls us to go, we cannot remain free. This is the life of faith.

Lust addicts, similar to Peter, are people who have had difficulty with restraint, deprivation and the limiting nature of commitments and choices. We want life to be open ended. Furthermore, because we believe we are especially bad or especially entitled, we have taken the easy way, insisting on our controlling ways, despite the dangers and consequences ahead. The root of this is the fear of death, the apparent ultimate blow to personal autonomy. This is part of what holds us "in lifelong bondage." Fearing the limits and deprivations of aging and death, the lust addict digs in his heals and asserts his false freedom, thus assuring bondage to lust addiction. This is what it means to be "held in lifelong bondage," to assert in the face of death my right to do as I wish.

Roy K, the founder of Sexaholics Anonymous, wrote a popular piece called The Luster's Fear of Dying. He wrote, "For the typical lust addict, our whole system screams out that we're going to die if we don't take that "drink." It's too fearful not to drink. Lust is our spiritual life-support system. Yes, the fear is that real. So, we wind up drinking. We're hooked on it and remain a slave. It's the fear of this kind of death that keeps us in bondage and forces us to keep slipping with lust." Lust addiction is a form of spiritual immaturity which believes against evidence, diminishing choices, aging, and death, that we create our own "eternal" life. Because sex is intimately connected with procreation and "possibilities," its dark cousin lust boasts that it can hold off even death itself. But like all spiritual attempts at "control," they are doomed to failure in the long run.

When I first got sober, several providential events became aligned. One of them was that I began to contemplate my advancing age. I heard a sobering lecture from a woman therapist who spoke of the "sin unto death." As addicts, we often delude ourselves to think we can quit "whenever we want to." The reality is that "way leads onto way" (Robert Frost) and we can find ourselves lurching toward death as practicing addicts. As mentioned previously, I had spent time in XXX movies earlier in my life and was surprised to see the theatre filed with grey and white haired men. This scene convinced me that if I did quit, it would not be because of age.

As in all recovery, after the resurrection, Peter had to undergo a restoration process (most likely shortened and summarized in John 21) that allowed him to accept the will of God as the life-blood of his very existence.

The fear of death which had previously held him in the bondage of self-protection was now gone.

Many of us have learned in recovery that there are no short-cuts and God does not settle for half-measures and half-hearted attempts, not if we really want to be free. Not if we are to make real progress. (Could this have been what Jesus meant by the "narrow way" and his startling claim that "few will find it?") The truly blessed are those who discover that God's will, though often not easy, is in fact their highest joy. Once recovery is a way of life, self-seeking short-cuts lose their appeal. Legend holds that the man who once refused to be captured was crucified upside down because he was not worthy to die like his Lord. Apparently, surrender to Jesus became his food and drink. Part of Peter's recovery may have been the contemplation of legacy, the understanding that the phrase "when you are old" brings to many. But letting go of the "fear of dying" which had held him is its cornerstone.

Though we never reach a perfect embrace of God's will in this life, the lust addict, through daily surrender and "progressive victory over lust" can find a deeper congruence between his or her will and God's. In an excerpt from the Big Book, Alcoholics Anonymous (page 63) the Third Step Prayer states:

God, I offer myself to Thee-
To build with me
and to do with me as Thou wilt.
Relieve me of the bondage of self,
that I may better do Thy will.
Take away my difficulties,
that victory over them may bear witness
to those I would help of Thy Power,
Thy Love, and Thy Way of life.
May I do Thy will always! 1

How is it possible to "go where you do not want to go?" Hebrews 11 answers that very question. In fact, it answers a more direct question. How can I accept by faith things that are not seen and promises not delivered in this life? How can I experience "the expulsive power of a new affection?" As previously mentioned, the lust addict tends to be focused on getting what he or she can in this life, so how can we possibly let go and trust that what God will give us in this life will be more than enough? How can we believe what awaits us in the next life will be infinitely better? How do we believe that "he rewards those who diligently seek him?" (Hebrews 11:6b) How can we believe that the life of recovery is superior to the life of addiction, a necessary step if we are not to be doomed to continual slipping?

The writer of Hebrews begins by saying that God has always done it this way. "..what is seen was not made out of things that are visible." If God created everything we see "out of nothing," then why is it difficult to believe the rewards, rest, and glory of the next world are any less assured? They too can be brought to existence "ex nihilo." (out of nothing) How can we believe this? How can this kind of faith become fully operational in us now?

The key verse in Hebrews 11 is verse 6. It governs and casts its force over the entire chapter. "And without faith it is impossible to please him, for whoever would draw near to God must first believe that he exists and that he rewards those who diligently seek him." The key to understanding this verse is to begin at the end. The writer is making a bold claim: To follow and love God, we must believe that He is and that he rewards us. We must believe that life with Him, including all that he has given us, both good and bad, is superior to that which we could have had without him. This is precisely what lust addicts like me have been unable to believe our whole lives until we surrendered in recovery. We wanted to grab and get instead of let go and receive.

How does this relate to us? Very simply, the lust addict cannot believe that God has given him or her enough. In our case, we often find ourselves chasing the next person or next image believing that somehow they will cure us or at least stop the addictive itch. This incessant activity takes place despite all evidence in our personal history proving that another person or image will never cure us. In this case, the unbelief occurs within us but is directed outward toward our addictive substance.

There exists a co-dependent aspect to all addiction. We are dependent on the substance of our addiction to continue functioning, that is, until "the party is over" and we come to truly believe that God will reward us apart from our addictive behavior. Until then, we will likely continue to lust and act out.

But what about same-sex attraction? One of the most common problems in some lust addicts who experience same-sex attraction is the stronghold of "envy" or "comparison." In the case of men, the person who experiences this believes that other men are better endowed, more manly, or more desirable 'as men" than they are. This is an entrenched belief inside them, often one that cannot be changed by telling them that they are mature, wise, good-looking or talented. This self-deprecation almost always gets in early through father-neglect or abuse or being given a standard to live up to as a man that is impossibly high. In the case of the "father-wound," this can produce a sexualized pursuit of a male figure, rather than coming to terms with the father loss, grieving it, forgiving and releasing one's father and finding healthy connections with men in the present. Regardless of the cause, the resulting pervasive feeling that remains is "I am not enough."

Also, because lust can be a way to receive affirmation, we often speak of "wanting to be lusted after" as the flip side of our own lust. But unless a person themselves "believes," by ultimately receiving God's affirmation, there can be no lasting change. The voice or presence of the denigrating or neglectful father, father-figure or influential person must be replaced by the affirming, loving presence of God, mediated by the supportive presence of healthy community. Men with a father wound need the healthy affirmation of other men. This is why atheists and agnostics who find themselves "in the rooms" due to addictive behavior often find that the presence of God and the grace-filled voice of other men to be very helpful in stilling the addictive pull.

Hebrews 11 is crucial for the lust addict. Until we can actually believe the God-life is more desirable and more worthy of our service, we cannot be free. This is why the belief of Step 2 (Came to believe that a power greater than ourselves could restore us to sanity) precedes the surrender of Step 3. So how does the writer of Hebrews make his case? He does it by telling stories of suffering Old Testament figures, many of whom wandered the earth "destitute, afflicted, mistreated." (Verse 37) These, he says, "died in faith not having received the things promised, having acknowledged that they were strangers and exiles on the earth." Despite their suffering, they were not crippled by fear nor "subject to lifelong bondage." They did not demand of this life more than it was designed to give. Instead, they walked in faith even though they had not received what was promised.

Well, if this God is a God who rewards his people, why didn't they get what they wanted on earth? Because God reserves the best for last. This is a great theme of the epistle and a reason why the "rest of God" is its theme. God "does away with the first order to establish the second." (Hebrews 10:9) Why didn't the groom at the wedding in Cana bring out the good wine first? (John 2: 10) Because, "you have kept the good wine until now." "Better is end of a thing than its beginning." (Ecclesiastes 7:8) This is the nature of the kingdom, promise and fulfillment. The last is better than the first. As Paul writes about Old Testament stories, Now these things happened to them as an example, but they were written down for our instruction, on whom the end of the ages has come." (1 Corinthians 10:11) We who are alive now participate in God's final plan for the world, and look forward joining together with those who in their earthly life "did not receive what was promised."

But the people who "died in faith" also did not want to settle for a physical homeland when an eternal one was being offered. They were not willing to sell their birthright for a hot meal. Why? Because while the latter was fleeting, the former was lasting. Because "people who speak thus make it clear they are seeking a homeland…But as it is, they desire a better country, that is a heavenly one." (Verse 16) This is where the lust addict, or any addict for that matter, is intrigued, to say the least. We are people who have been looking for the "better country" all our lives. We have also seen through our own drives that the addictive substance, no matter what it is, cannot deliver the "better country" of enduring rest and peace. "Therefore God is not ashamed to be called their God, for he has prepared for them a city." Our hunger and thirst is a sign that something exists beyond this life that will satisfy it one day.

Have you ever asked yourself why God loves the wanderer, the sojourner, the seeker, the desperate, lonely and restless? Because their need and vulnerability creates room for God. Jesus said to Zacchaeus the wealthy but despised tax collector, "Zacchaeus, hurry and come down, for I must stay at your house today." (Luke 19:5) He "must" come to Zacchaeus to satisfy his hungry heart. "Yet the LORD longs to be gracious to you; therefore he will rise up to show you compassion." (Isaiah 30:18a) But there is more. The writer simply cannot control himself with the endless accounts of living "by faith" in light of the promise of rest to come.

32 And what more shall I say? For time would fail me to tell of Gideon, Barak, Samson, Jephthah, of David and Samuel and the prophets—33 who through faith conquered kingdoms, enforced justice, obtained promises, stopped the mouths of lions, 34 quenched the power of fire, escaped the edge of the sword, were made strong out of weakness, became mighty in war, put foreign armies to flight. 35 Women received back their dead by resurrection. Some were tortured, refusing to accept release, so that they might rise again to a better life. 36 Others suffered mocking and flogging, and even chains and imprisonment. 37 They were stoned, they were sawn in two,[a] they were killed with the sword. They went about in skins of sheep and goats, destitute, afflicted, mistreated—38 of whom the world was not worthy—wandering about in deserts and mountains, and in dens and caves of the earth.

39 And all these, though commended through their faith, did not receive what was promised, 40 since God had provided something better for us, that apart from us they should not be made perfect. (Hebrews 11:32-40)

The experience spoken about in this passage was so powerful in the first two centuries of the Christian church that many believers began seeking martyrdom, so much so that the church had to issue "cease and desist" messages urging believers to understand that God might have a plan for them in this world before passing onto the next.

Hebrews 11 is a bold passage for 21st century Jesus followers to contemplate. The writer informs us that we stand in a long line of people of who didn't fully receive in this world what God has promised. So what then is the appeal of this kind of talk to the lust addicted? How can it give us hope, empower us to let go of the things that drive us and embrace the "better country"?

First of all, we must understand how privileged we are as people of the New Covenant. We have Jesus, his words, his finished work, his resurrection power, his interceding presence, and his "...his precious and very great promises," (2 Peter 1:4). But these promises are not just words or abstract theological thoughts. They have a specific purpose:. "... So that through them you may become partakers of the divine nature, having escaped from the corruption that is in the world because of sinful desire." (ie lust). We have the Holy Spirit, the body of Christ, Christian books, supportive ministries, and if we are fortunate, prayerful and listening friends and much more. The writer is pointing to a necessary truth. Not only do we have it better than these Old Testament characters. They are counting on us to walk "by faith" so that the one people of God will be united in the heavenly city. What is happening to us is the fulfillment of God's promise to them. We have a legacy and a calling that unites the generations if we are willing to embrace it. When a lust addict enters sobriety and recovery, they are not just personally recovering for their own benefit. What they have done and continue to do will influence other lust addicts, not to mention their marriages, children, family tree, church, community and beyond.

Our faithfulness is desperately needed today to keep the unbreakable bond between the faithful of previous generations and "the church militant here in earth." When the addict understands he or she is bound to something greater, a breakthrough can often occur. When Bill W. understood he must help another alcoholic in order to stay sober, he began to understand the common bond of the addicted if only for his own generation. When we discover that helping others helps us, this is when the we find a purpose to move beyond addiction to significance. I feel sorry for those who leave 12 Step programs feeling that "I don't need it any more." Well, recovery is not just about us. It is about the next hurting person who walks in the door. He or she needs our experience, strength and hope to stay sober. We are bound up with others in the bundle of life (1 Samuel 25:29) because the fulfilling of the promises given to these renowned Old Testament figures and unknown sojourners "apart from us" will not be realized. The baton has been passed to us. And how we run the race matters more than we can imagine.

We are more dependent on each other than we know. A significant contributor to sexual addiction is the inner belief deep inside the addict that he or she stands "apart." This secretive life is buttressed by a false sense of entitlement, shame or fear that often keeps us isolated, resentful and lonely. But when the lust addict comes out of the shadows and into the light, we begin to see not only that we belong but that others are counting on us. Not only so, we see over time that we all need others to stand by us or even pick us up off the ground from time to time. Amazingly, some us who are picked up by sheer grace eventually return the favor to others when their moment comes. No wonder people say "My recovery is the most important thing in my life." It is the prism through which we see all of life.

We are bound up with one another in ways we cannot fully appreciate at the moment. When I first changed careers and went into the financial services business, I was living a high pressure existence, My stress-o-meter was flashing red. Then things got worse. I got so physically sick that I had to stay home for four months. This was like a boxer rising from the canvass only to be knocked down again. One day I went into my boss's office to engage in a difficult conversation. I told him, "I am not sure I can continue with this job. I am so far behind. Maybe I should quit." In that moment, I heard one of the most gracious and empowering statements I have ever heard. My boss said, "Well if you need to quit or do something else for a while, feel free to do it.

But know this. If you want to work here again, you can come back any time. I will hire you back whenever you want because I believe in you." These were the words I needed to hear. Somehow I got through the transition and flourished in the years ahead. Subsequently, that same boss went through a very difficult time of his own. I was able to come alongside him and encourage him in his time of trouble. We are friends to this day.

This is the beauty, reciprocity and unity of the community of recovery, one that is more authentic and fulfilling than on-line false connections. One of the great wonders in addiction recovery is watching the broken addict rise and begin to help, encourage and support those who are struggling with their same problem. This was apparently a significant part of the early church's ministry focus. As the Apostle Paul writes,

[3] Blessed be the God and Father of our Lord Jesus Christ, the Father of mercies and God of all comfort, [4] who comforts us in all our affliction, so that we may be able to comfort those who are in any affliction, with the comfort with which we ourselves are comforted by God. (2 Corinthians 1:3). Thus, when we see that giving, not getting, is the road to freedom, we just may begin to walk this path on a consistent basis. This desire is expressed in The Prayer of St. Francis, used as the 11th Step Prayer.

Lord, make me an instrument of Your peace. Where there is hatred, let me sow love; where there is injury, pardon; where there is doubt, faith; where there is despair, hope; where there is darkness, light; where there is sadness, joy.

O, Divine Master, grant that I may not so much seek to be consoled as to console; to be understood as to understand; to be loved as to love; For it is in giving that we receive; it is in pardoning that we are pardoned; it is in dying that we are born again to eternal life. Amen.

How then does the lust addict face death? If we are to be free, we must let go of concupiscence, the desire to possess and control either images or other people. The "fear of death" for the lust addict, which subjects us "to lifelong bondage" is the desire to control and enjoy lust. We will never be free while indulging lust. For us this means believing that God is doing for us what we cannot do for ourselves, that surrendering our will and life to him on a daily basis is the path of freedom, that where we are going is a better, more fulfilling existence than attempting to hang onto the things of this world. Asking this world to fulfill us in ways it was never designed to always leads to despair. Letting go, serving and loving others, becoming agents in his redeeming work with other addicts: These are the things that truly make us part of God's plan of "reconciling all things in heaven and on earth." (Colossians 1:20) The early AA's called this Step 12. "Having had a spiritual awakening as a result of these steps, we tried to carry this message to other alcoholics and to practice these principles in all our affairs."1

Eleven

Finishing Strong: Resentment, Lust, Discipline and Love

*Everything in the world is more or less misunderstood at first:
we have to learn what it is, and come at length to see that it
must be so, that it could not be otherwise. Then we know it;
and we never know a thing really until we know it thus.*

George MacDonald

*Progressive revelation of our defective
self is a sign of true recovery.*

Ron J.

15 *See to it that no one fails to obtain the grace of God;
that no "root of bitterness" springs up and causes trouble,
and by it many become defiled;* **16** *that no one is sexually
immoral or unholy like Esau, who sold his birthright for
a single meal.* **17** *For you know that afterward, when he
desired to inherit the blessing, he was rejected, for he found
no chance to repent, though he sought it with tears.*

(Hebrews 12:15-17)

135

Other than Jesus' own teaching concerning lust in Matthew 5:27-28, Hebrews 12:15-17 is likely the key passage in the Bible that unveils the deeper issues in sex addiction. Particularly, the issue of "bitterness" rises to the top, along with its twin "resentment." A businessman friend of mine once described these twin character defects as "writing out invoices against other people." When we do this, we are saying inside ourselves, "Pay me what you owe me." The list of things people owe a resentful person is virtually endless, money, attention, forgiveness, time, love, preferment and the list goes on. Many people live their lives in a continuous spiritual bother which burns inside them, an agitation which roots them in the belief they are being mistreated, misunderstood, under-appreciated or excluded. It seems to be a spirit that enters into our souls, one that for some remains lifelong. This is not an ancillary condition but rather a foundational spiritual illness. The writer of Hebrews calls it a "root." Although this "root of bitterness" may be caused by a "series of unfortunate events" because some lives experience more woe than others; it also seems to be based on our reaction to these events. We all know people with difficult backgrounds who are grateful and generous despite their personal histories. We also know people from privileged and relatively unscathed families who are bitter and resentful. The root of bitterness is more about our reaction to events than the events themselves. If left unresolved, this spiritual condition can continually feed the cycle of addiction as the addict attempts to medicate themselves from the inner badness of resentment.

Of course, we are all spoken against, mistreated or excluded from time to time. This is part of the human experience. But those possessed by the root of bitterness often find it to be their go-to emotion, their processing filter for much of reality. They look for ways to feel "less than." They feel rejected at the slightest oversight even when no one is actually rejecting them and as a result live their lives with internal pain which often manifests itself as a chip on the shoulder. One of the most noteworthy portrayals of this in literature is the title character from Thomas Hardy's The Mayor of Casterbridge, a classic portrayal of the resentful alcoholic. He sells his wife and daughter to another man at a country fair, and proceeds to walk through life embittered because other people are not acting in the way he believes they should. Though difficult to watch, I highly recommend the BBC's video version starring Alan Bates. The writer of Hebrews indicates that this kind of unresolved bitterness can defile "the many." It certainly impacts those who live with someone determined to look on the negative side of life.

But to drill down on the passage we must ask why was Esau "unholy" and what this has to do with being "sexually immoral?" If you remember, Esau comes in from the field (Genesis 25:29) and is hungry. When our appetites warp our perspective, food, drink and sex can often be the culprits driving us to sell our souls. This is the famous HALT mechanism, (Hungry Angry Lonely Tired) and it continues to keep people off balance in the 21st century. In this case the manipulative Jacob, the "supplanter," sees an opening to seize what was not his, namely the birthright given to the eldest son. Esau, blinded by his hunger, is only too willing to give up this precious gift for the pleasure of the moment, in this case a hot meal.

The writer of Hebrews is telling us that the same spirit that drove Esau to sacrifice long-term identity for short-term pleasure is the same spirit that drives immorality. I can distinctly remember a time in my life when I was mistreated vocationally. In my mind, I was rejected, dealt with unjustly and ignored. Within a period of weeks, I was acting out. Having not been given something I think I deserved made me determined to grab and take.

The writer makes the comparison between sexual immorality and hunger. Both can lead us to medicate in the short term, engage in "unholy" activity and sacrifice greater long-term concerns and goals. But which comes first the indulgence or the resentment? It doesn't really matter. Once the "go to" addiction is set up in the person's life, as a response to perceived slights, the connection between the two is what matters, not which comes first. They are, in fact, mutually reinforcing. In the case of Esau, the indulgence comes first. He ate the hot meal. In Genesis 25:34, we are told, "Then Esau despised his birthright." Having sold it and consumed the meal, he then belittled its value. "I didn't want it anyway. It doesn't matter." This is resentment following indulgence. Having engaged in our addiction, we will often resent the consequences that follow. We will object to the reaping of what we have sown. The overeater or binge eater goes into a downward spiral underpinned by a "what's the use" attitude. The porn addict similarly can slide downhill, believing they are beyond help and hope. Unless this process is interrupted by a multi-faceted recovery program, they can be swept into a negatively reinforcing cycle. Indulgence followed by resentment leads to medicating the resentment by indulging again. This is the "body of death" from which the Apostle Paul asked, "Who will deliver me?" (Romans 7:24)

Addiction is a spiritual illness. Accordingly, it pervades every part of a person's life, relationships, attitudes, beliefs and conduct. Just as recovery can produce the fruit of a positive spirituality, so addiction can produce alienation from God and man. This is why addiction always impacts relationships.

The desired outcome of lust recovery is not simply a cessation of lust but a transformation of all relationships, attitudes and conduct. This is why Steps 4 and 5 which unearth our wrongs, Steps 6 and 7 which ask God to free us from specific character defects and change us and Steps 8 and 9 which call for amends to others we have hurt, are so critical to the restoration and transformation of the individual. When followed, "the wreckage of the past" can truly be cleaned up in remarkable ways and the possibility of returning to "wallow in the mire" is greatly reduced.

The context of this passage is to "run with endurance the race that is set before us, looking to Jesus the founder and perfecter of our faith." (Hebrews 12:2a) Having been a long-distance runner myself, there is nothing more free and unencumbered than a fully-trained, lightly dressed and shod runner fully given to run his course. This is Jesus's desire for us as his followers. Psalm 19 expresses similar sentiments concerning "the heavens."

In them he has set a tent for the sun,
   5 which comes out like a bridegroom leaving his chamber,
    and, like a strong man, runs its course with joy. (Psalm 19:5)

These words speak of the enabling power of a "bridegroom" openly relating to his wife, free of addictive compulsion. Similarly Hebrews 12 speaks of Jesus as our forerunner, our example and our destination, the true bridegroom who has run ahead and prepared a place for us, his bride. But to run our race, we must "lay aside every weight and sin which clings so closely." (Verse 1b) What specifically are these weights and sins?

The writer tells us that one of these is discouragement due to undergoing God's discipline. "My son, do not make light of the Lord's discipline and do not lose heart when he rebukes you... (Hebrews 12:5b NIV)). One of the most difficult parts of the recovery process from sexual addiction is when the recovering addict has ceased their behaviors and is actively doing many if not most of the things he or she needs to become healthy again. The difficulty lies in the fact that many of the feel-good fruits of recovery may not have actually materialized yet.

In the beginning, the process of recovery is like a slow moving car accident. There is the skid, the crash, the finding out who is hurt and then all the events surrounding physical, emotional and spiritual recovery, not to mention repairing or replacing the car. This takes a long time. The recovering addict may likely not receive instantaneous forgiveness from those he or she has hurt. Even if we do, emotional distancing from family and friends is a natural consequence for a while. We may experience legal, medical or vocational challenges. Unfortunately, having denied the inevitability of consequences most of our lives, we may approach recovery with a "hurry up" attitude. Many an addict has wished for their spouse to "get over it," when the spouse has just begun to process all that has occurred. Many therapists advise that when betrayal is discovered, a minimum of six months must pass before anger begins to subside from violated spouses. This can lead to discouragement. Why won't my wife forgive me? Why can't I find a job? Why can't I see my kids more? Why have most of my friends abandoned me? There is real temptation to become discouraged or to surrender to fear about trusting God for the future. This is the very problem addressed by Hebrews 12, even though it also applies to innocent suffering.

Persistent and ongoing challenges dished out by life can produce hopelessness. "Drooping hands" and "weak knees" (Verse 12) are physical signs of it. In times like these, we need people close to us who will hold us up and continually speak into our lives the hope that things can get better. When I first got into recovery in 1993 and was experiencing difficult times, I spent half my days looking for work and half my days on my recovery program, working steps, praying, journaling, attending meetings and reading. In early days, attention to recovery and establishing a new direction is absolutely essential. So is finding one or two friends who will stand by our side. We cannot recover alone.

Often we run into a problem. If things we hope will change don't, then resentment can metastasize into a "root of bitterness." There are things we cannot change, even though as Esau did, we seek them "with tears." Our spouse decides to divorce us. We can't find a job. Friendships vanish, never to be resurrected. We then begin to make unwarranted sweeping conclusions such as "life is against me or there is no way I will ever recover from this." Oddly, these thoughts can even take place within us when "life" is the result of our own bad choices. Having hidden our secret existence, once the dam has burst, it can feel like the flood will never stop. All the more necessary to establish even the rudiments of a positive direction. For those of us in ministry accustomed to doing "great things for God," we will need to adjust our expectations. A meeting with a supportive friend over coffee, a first job interview or a cool afternoon walk or run may be the new standard of "a good day." Having fended pain off for decades, sometimes "It is better to go to the house of mourning than to go to the house of feasting." (Ecclesiastes 7:2a). Writing in a journal and processing our feelings may be just the thing we need.

In times like this, Hebrews 12: 7-11 are key verses. They give us a peek into the process that God is up to, providing us with the faith and hope we need to see it through.

" It is for discipline that you have to endure. God is treating you as sons. For what son is there whom his father does not discipline? [8] If you are left without discipline, in which all have participated, then you are illegitimate children and not sons. ⁹ Besides this, we have had earthly fathers who disciplined us and we respected them. Shall we not much more be subject to the Father of spirits and live? ¹⁰ For they disciplined us for a short time as it seemed best to them, but he disciplines us for our good, that we may share his holiness. ¹¹ For the moment all discipline seems painful rather than pleasant, but later it yields the peaceful fruit of righteousness to those who have been trained by it."

The writer helps us understand that the entire process of restoration, of discipline if you like, is a sign of our being children of God, even when it feels like an arbitrary, random or even hurtful process. What an important perspective this is! It's very presence and forward movement, far from being some kind of punishment or banishment, is a sign of God's investment in us as his children, of his deep and abiding love. Part of this process is God pulling out the "root of bitterness" and replacing it with the fruit of the Spirit which will grow over time. If you are reading this and you are in the early stages of recovery and restoration, hold on. As the Big Book says,

"If we are painstaking about this phase of our development we will be amazed before we are half way through. We are going to know a new freedom and a new happiness. We will not regret the past nor wish to shut the door on it. We will comprehend the word serenity and we will know peace. No matter how far down the scale we have gone, we will see how our experience can benefit others. That feeling of uselessness and self-pity will disappear. We will lose interest in selfish things and gain interest in our fellows. Self-seeking will slip away. Our whole attitude and outlook upon life will change. Fear of people and economic insecurity will leave us. We will intuitively know how to handle situations which used to baffle us. We will suddenly realize that God is doing for us what we could not do for ourselves. Are these extravagant Promises? We think not. They are being fulfilled among us - sometimes quickly, sometimes slowly. They will always materialize if we work for them." Alcoholics Anonymous, p. 83-84)1

For the sex addict in the early stages of recovery, these words are golden because they point to progress that we cannot yet see. Hope is kindled. Don't grow "weary or fainthearted." (Verse3) Your life is about to get much better if you see it through. Just remember, you are not in control of it and He "has done all things well." (Mark 7:37). He will see you through. God is not giving us our old life back. That is gone forever. Rather, he is giving us a new life we have never experienced, one that is better than we could possibly imagine.

We are learning that self-will had been our enemy at the same time God had wanted to be our friend. We are making room for Jesus. Remember the "Behold I stand at the door and knock" passage where

Jesus asks entrance in Revelation 3:20? It was directed at the church, to believing people. Specifically, we are to keep in mind these truths. First, discipline is a sign of our being God's children and his investment in us. (Verses 7 and 8). If I have learned one thing in recovery it is that he never gives up on us. Ever. He not only leaves the ninety-nine to go after the one. "Just so, I tell you, there will be more joy in heaven over one sinner who repents than over ninety-nine righteous persons who need no repentance." (Luke 15:7) He loves to do it. As the story of the prodigal son in Luke 15 illustrates, God wants to throw a party over us as he sweeps us up in his arms. All we have to do is to "come to ourselves" and come home.

Secondly, God's discipline process is worthy of our respect and cooperation. Why? Because his restoration process is infinitely better and more thorough than our earthly father's could ever be. It is part and parcel of our "sonship." You see we all have something of the "father wound." God or our father let us down and we have never been the same since. But the core message of the New Testament, our own sonship with the Father, is the answer, the healing balm we seek. And in that healing he asks us to trust him again. There may be times when we doubt what is going on because we don't see the whole picture. But Jesus sees it and knows what he is doing. If we do not get discouraged and stop, good things will come to pass. Keep working the program no matter what.

Thirdly, we are told these earthly fathers disciplined us "for a short time, but he disciplines us for our good." (Verse10) Our earthly fathers took care of us only during our childhood. They may have done it for the purpose of manners and morals or for a whole variety of reasons. If we were fortunate, they did it out of love and a desire to serve our long-term good. But God does it for our eternal betterment so that we "might share his holiness." (Verse10) There is a far greater and more eternal purpose to God's discipline than we know, making it more valuable and desirable than the best human father's. His purpose is that we might share his very nature throughout all eternity.

Finally, the unpleasant and difficult nature of this kind of discipline does pass. A pastor friend of mine says, "It did not come to stay. It came to pass." Whatever pain you may be experiencing due to consequences of your behavior and the difficult awakening through the initial stages of recovery, the pain will pass. And what will be left? A precious harvest. "The peaceful fruit of righteousness." We have all seen an out of control child, throwing tantrums and violating boundaries with a vengeance. Then the parent enters and exercises appropriate discipline with love. The child then becomes peaceful and quiet. There is a peace that comes when this restoration is complete. The best part is that real recovery becomes a permanent part of our character and way of life. Even through slips and restarts, we can never go back to the way things were, because we do not choose to. Through recovery, it can truly be said of us:

"What no eye has seen, nor ear heard,
    nor the heart of man imagined,
what God has prepared for those who love him"— (1 Corinthians 2:9)

An Invitation: Which Mountaintop?

In the movie Chariots of Fire, Harold Abrahams, played superbly by Ben Cross, is an ambitious Jew who fights the Christian Anglo-Saxon establishment in England he perceives is blocking him from "the corridors of power." In a moment of confrontation with two Cambridge masters, Abrahams asserts his athletic professionalism. "I will carry the future with me," he says. The Trinity Master, played by John Gielgud responds with a sigh. "There goes your Semite, Hugh. A different God, a different mountaintop."

The writer of Hebrews is not interested in anti-Semitic one-upmanship. But he is interested in the contrast between Mount Sinai and Mount Zion. In Exodus 20, at Mt. Sinai, we read "the people stood far off" because "they could not endure the order that was given." (Hebrews 12:20) The event, the giving of the law, was filled "with fear" (Verse 21), even for Moses. Why does the writer include this passage here? I believe it is because he wants to make sure his readers understand that the discipline they may be experiencing is not a re-imposition of the law. It is not punishment. The difficulties they are experiencing do not represent a return to the reinforcing bind of law and sin that so characterized life in temple worship. Whatever discipline they endure now is not a never-ending replay of the shame of sin and addiction, the endless wash, rinse, repeat of the addictive cycle, one that "can never take away sins." (Hebrews 10:4). There is a different kind of shaking going on, one that is redemptive and focused on eternity, not one that is condemnatory resulting in distancing from God. So what is the word from Mt. Zion? According to Hebrews it is a voice that "warns from heaven." (Hebrews 12:25). The writer contrasts it with the voice that "warned them on earth," in other words from Mt Sinai. The heavenly word like the heavenly city is more comforting, more reliable, more sure, more permanent. "Yet once more I will shake not only the earth but the heavens." (Verse 26) What is the purpose of this shaking? Not to promote fear or judgment or distancing. No, it is "in order that the things that cannot be shaken may remain." (Verse 27) The shaking of the impermanent focuses us on the eternal, as anyone who has lost their house to fire or earthquake will tell you. People standing in the rubble of their houses in television interviews inevitably speak of their newfound focus on higher things. Property can be replaced, people cannot.

There are things in us God is still working on. If so, then the sooner we let go of the things that bind us and allow them to be shaken from us, the better. The pursuit of fame, power, wealth and pleasure are some of these things that bind us. After all, eventually our earthly "tents" and finally our last breath will be shaken from us as we prepare for the next world. Until then, we simply bear with the process as God removes in us "the things that are shaken." The "consuming fire" (Verse 29) does not remove us. Unlike Sinai which revealed a fiery earth that swallowed up the disobedient, Zion merely burns from us the things that continue to hold us in this world.

Every addict of every kind can relate to these words, even the person with decades of sobriety and recovery. They serve to counteract the small seductive voice that still attempts to convince us that a portion of our addictive substance might be ok to use today. Instead, we have accepted that in the process of being "shaken" and our defects "consumed," God is calling us to let go.

Twelve

From Here to Eternity: The Measure of a Recovering Addict

But the path of the righteous is like the light of dawn,
which shines brighter and brighter until full day.

Proverbs 4:18

O God, support us all the day long,
until the shadows lengthen and the evening comes,
and the busy world is hushed,
and the fever of life is over,
and our work is done.
Then in your mercy grant us a safe lodging
And a holy rest
And peace at the last
Through Jesus Christ our Savior. Amen.

John Henry Newman

Let brotherly love continue. [2] Do not neglect to show hospitality to strangers, for thereby some have entertained angels unawares.[3]

Remember those who are in prison, as though in prison with them, and those who are mistreated, since you also are in the body. [4] Let marriage be held in honor among all, and let the marriage bed be undefiled, for God will judge the sexually immoral and adulterous. [5] Keep your life free from love of money, and be content with what you have, for he has said, "I will never leave you nor forsake you." [6] So we can confidently say,

"The Lord is my helper;
   I will not fear;
what can man do to me?"

[7] Remember your leaders, those who spoke to you the word of God. Consider the outcome of their way of life, and imitate their faith. [8] Jesus Christ is the same yesterday and today and forever. [9] Do not be led away by diverse and strange teachings, for it is good for the heart to be strengthened by grace, not by foods, which have not benefited those devoted to them. [10] We have an altar from which those who serve the tent have no right to eat. [11] For the bodies of those animals whose blood is brought into the holy places by the high priest as a sacrifice for sin are burned outside the camp. [12] So Jesus also suffered outside the gate in order to sanctify the people through his own blood. [13] Therefore let us go to him outside the camp and bear the reproach he endured. [14] For here we have no lasting city, but we seek the city that is to come. [15] Through him then let us continually offer up a sacrifice of praise to God, that is, the fruit of lips that acknowledge his name. [16] Do not neglect to do good and to share what you have, for such sacrifices are pleasing to God.

[17] Obey your leaders and submit to them, for they are keeping watch over your souls, as those who will have to give an account. Let them do this with joy and not with groaning, for that would be of no advantage to you. (Hebrews 13: 1-17)

At first reading, Hebrews 13 appears to leave the theme of resentment elucidated in detail in chapter 12 and move on to various exhortations regarding practical Christian behavior. But this is not true. The exhortations of Hebrews 13 are a direct result of surrendering resentment. Notice also that the writer mentions other kinds of lust, namely freedom from the "love of money." These are specific "letting go" behaviors characteristic of the believer living in freedom from lust addiction.

As previously mentioned, 2 Peter is concerned about believers being "effective" and "fruitful" as Christians, by building specific virtues into their lives, serving and so on. Similarly, the writer of Hebrews is convinced that specific action is needed to walk out all that God has for us. Lust addicts who take these actions will build spiritual qualities into their lives that prevent the dual dangers of resentment and lust from invading and defiling their souls once again. How do we do this? We do it by working a 12 Step program in its entirety. We attend regular meetings, we work steps, and surrender character defects. We take on others to sponsor, do service, read literature, study Scripture. As we do these things, these virtues literally become ours.

Loving Others

The first fruit of recovery is a desire to give to others. Indeed, as Bill W discovered and as we have mentioned repeatedly here, he could not remain sober unless he helped other alcoholics. His incident in the Mayflower Hotel in Akron, where he was compelled to find another alcoholic to help or he would drink again, cemented forever the understanding that the best way to help ourselves is to help others. Many today misunderstand God's action in light of the belief that we must always receive God's love first before we can love others. This may be true in the initial stages of our relationship with God. We therefore conclude that in every circumstance receiving love is primary, while loving others follows.

God's love does come first in the scheme of salvation. We love because he first loved us. (1 John 4:19) Our ethos and practice is a response to his love. But in terms of our daily discipline, we are to love others first. We are to initiate and not wait to be loved by them. This is the very atmosphere of the kingdom, initiating, action-oriented love. So, the writer of Hebrews says, "Let brotherly love continue." The only way a lust addict can continue to be free is to help others, serve and listen to others. Recently I was watching a 60 Minutes interview with a grizzled Marine officer who was responsible for informing future Gold Star parents that their son or daughter had been killed in action. He spoke about his final doorstep knock at a house in Kansas around dinner time. As he informed the family that their son had been killed in action, the mother, dressed in an apron, asked him twice if he would like to stay for dinner. Both times the marine officer declined. With tears in his eyes, he informed the interviewer that he deeply regretted his refusal. "You see," he said, "They just wanted to tell me about their son." Listening to others is part of taking the actions of love.

So for us, as we recover and to insure our continued recovery, we must love and give and serve others. Giving is not optional. Neither is being available. Loving others will differ according to our gifts and passions but it will never be optional. We must love and give or we will return to our folly. Because we are never "cured" in this life, we must guard against self-pity, resentment and fear, all of which make us reticent to love.

Let the Marriage Bed Be Undefiled

Many have interpreted this warning as a call to refrain from adultery and fornication. Yes, but it is more than that. As John Paul II and others have pointed out, lust can also defile marriage. It does so when euphoric recall or pornographic images intrude into the marital bed. If, as Jesus said, adultery occurs when we have "lusted," then there is a deeper issue than genital sexual sin, fornication or adultery. Our lustful thought life too must be surrendered and eliminated if the marriage bed is to remain "undefiled." These struggles are subsumed under "sexually immoral." If lust is the problem, as Jesus asserted it was, then a married person lusting after another image or person is something he calls us to surrender to him. All of this is designed for our freedom, the "glorious liberty of the children of God," to which we have a foretaste if not actual possession in this life. Those of us who are surrendering lust in the marriage bed are discovering a deeper intimacy with our spouses than we have otherwise known.

Remember Your Leaders

Lust addicts have a problem with other people. A recent article on the history of European existentialists in the mid 20th century revealed a great deal of sexual immorality permeated the movement. No wonder. One of their leading writers, John Paul Sartre, once said, "Hell is other people." We lust addicts are more than familiar with the resentment-lust connection. Where there is one, the other is likely to be present. James says, "For where jealousy and selfish ambition exist, there will be disorder and every vile practice." (James 3:16) Fueling the "other people" problem is the fact that we often think of ourselves as better or worse than others. Too rarely do we think of ourselves as just like everyone else. Sometimes, we have a problem with authority figures. This happens for a number of reasons. We may think we know better or have more experience than our boss or our pastor or our parent. We may be jealous of their position. We may simply exhibit arrogant tendencies as one of our many character defects. Unacknowledged or unsurrendered, our attitudes toward others can drive us toward our addiction. What is the antidote to it?

Regarding spiritual leaders, we are called to "respect those who labor among you and are over you in the Lord and admonish you, [13] and to esteem them very highly in love because of their work. (I Thessalonians 5:12-13.) Specifically Hebrews tells us to "remember your leaders, those who spoke to you the word of God. Consider the outcome of their life and imitate their faith." (Hebrews 13:7). Rather than evaluate our leaders, we might turn the light on ourselves and ask some important questions.. Are we an irritant, a source of discord and negative attention to our leaders? Or are we a focus of reliability, support and encouragement, a force for unity and growth in the body of Christ? Can we be called upon in an emergency to sacrifice without recognition when the need arises? Notice, this is what is required "because of their work." It is the work that is important. We are to "esteem them highly in love." If you want to promote unity in the body of Christ and see your leaders flourish, love and affirm them without requiring excessive attention from them. It will be a gift to them as well as you, keeping you free from the poison of resentment. Kingdom work is all important and must go forward as unhindered as possible by our character defects. Actively affirming and supporting leaders helps pave the way for our continuing freedom. When tempted to self-pity, the Apostle Paul reminded both Timothy and himself,

"Remember Jesus Christ, risen from the dead, the offspring of David, as preached in my gospel, 9 for which I am suffering, bound with chains as a criminal. But the word of God is not bound!" (2 Timothy 2: 8-9) The Apostle Paul never forgot that the work was more important than he was. Principles before personalities.

Do we wonder if Christian service is worth it? Do we fret about the ultimate blessings of the Christian life in times of depression or uncertainty? If so, we can look to the lives of those who have served him, learn from their positive example and find strength and hope. Sometimes we need to thank those who brought the saving word of God to us. No one who has served God in this way ever received too much encouragement in a calling that has more than its share of discouragement. Early in our ministry, my wife and I engaged in a long and somewhat frustrating ministry with a woman alcoholic. After some time, she let go and became sober. For years, even after we left the church we served, she sent us gifts and notes of thanks. As far as we know, she remains sober to this day. What is that worth?

We often forget that a negative vibe can exist in ministry as people tend to come forward when something goes wrong in their lives or when they have a beef with us. How important then to affirm and follow positive examples in the body of Christ. As we do, we can then receive the Apostle Paul's words as people free of ego and selfish ambition. "I urge you then, be imitators of me." (1 Corinthians 4:16)

Don't Get Seduced by The New and Different

Why would the author of Hebrews teach that "Jesus Christ is the same, yesterday, today and forever?" (Verse 8) He tells us. "Do not be led away by diverse and strange teachings, for it is good for the heart to be strengthened by grace, not by foods which have not benefited those devoted to them." (Verses 9-10) Outcomes matter. This is why the writer has told us to imitate the lives of leaders. Many of us have thought that the newest book, teaching, seminar, worship style, video or prophetic utterance would save us. We wanted to take the easier, more ecstatic road and believe some new principle or way of thinking would automatically change us, without our hearts being changed or having to surrender our wills. I have learned that God respects humanity so much that he will not normally over-ride our choices, particularly in areas where surrender is required before freedom is enjoyed. Jesus is after our hearts, but sometimes we would rather surrender anything but our hearts, particularly hearts captivated by lust.

Many of us have learned painfully over time that the heart dominates the will and the mind. Salesmen tell us that people buy with their hearts and then justify the purchase with their minds and wills. According to Thomas Cranmer's, (an English reformer who wrote the first two Book(s) of Common Prayer) anthropology, "What the heart loves, the will chooses, and the mind justifies. The mind doesn't direct the will. The mind is actually captive to what the will wants, and the will itself, in turn, is captive to what the heart wants." (September 2001, *Anglican Church League News* interview with Dr. Ashley Null) Until the heart is changed, all abstract theologies, teachings and systems of thought are powerless to bring about lasting change in us. Unless God has our hearts, he does not have us.

We lust addicts are people who habitually believed that "the next one would save us." In our addiction, it was the next person or the next image that would fix us. As mentioned previously, this syndrome also relates to the belief that the next truth or movement of God also will save us, a kind of "deus ex machina" that instantly extricates us from long-standing problems. Furthermore, the whole "next" culture which drives the internet is also related to the "geographical cure." It goes like this: If I can simply move somewhere else or find a new spouse or lover, I will suddenly be free of the things that have driven me like the wind. As we know, this usually leads to disappointment. In recovery, we say, "Wherever you go, there you are." Easy fixes and external changes rarely help. So what are we to do?

In recovery, we respond to the easy fix temptation by saying, "Stick with the winners" (i.e. those whose long term recovery you respect) or "Stick with what works." To strengthen our faith and freedom, following Jesus and the 12 Step program of recovery is what works. We don't need a new Savior, a new spouse or a new place to live. We need a new heart. And he can give it to us.

Endure Persecution

In our addiction, many of us believed we had to be loved, admired, respected, even adored. Unfortunately, many enter ordained ministry with this attitude, not realizing that being in the spotlight can cut both ways. Many of us could not embrace both supportive friendship which we needed and the persecution or rejection which sometimes came our way. When opposed, we believed something was wrong with us. When criticized legitimately, we could not handle it. It did not help that because of our addiction, we knew, while others did not, what was lurking deep down inside us. After all, if our critics really knew what was wrong with us, they could really go to town, so we had to defend ourselves, cover up and get them off our trail quickly. The best way to do this was to defend, deny and object to any criticism. This is why maintaining equilibrium while indulging lust is so difficult. In recovery, we need a new perspective on persecution and the writer of Hebrews provides it.

[12] So Jesus also suffered outside the gate in order to sanctify the people through his own blood. [13] Therefore let us go to him outside the camp and bear the reproach he endured. [14] For here we have no lasting city, but we seek the city that is to come. (Hebrews 13:12-14)

Here are some important truths for all Christians but especially those addicted to the opinions of others. The point of Jesus suffering "outside the camp" is that the bodies of animals burned there were considered "unclean." Jesus, as the bearer of our sins was considered "unclean." He was willing to so identify with us that he became unclean for us. He "became sin for us." (II Corinthians 5:21)

The writer of Hebrews speaks of Jesus as living even today "outside the camp." Thus the exhortation to "go to him outside the camp and bear his reproach," is a calling to live with him where he dwells. Similarly, Jesus took pains to let a man know who would have followed him that "the Son of man has nowhere to lay his head." (Luke 9:58) Following him would be difficult. So the modern disciple must understand that Jesus lives in the place of shame and suffering to redeem those captured by them...outside the camp. Our recoiling from persecution is nothing less than unwillingness to identify with Jesus and share in his shame-bearing role. Where does this leave us when we embrace recovery, honesty and healing? When accused, we either admit the accusation as true, an opportunity for confession and repentance or if false we go outside the camp to Jesus and share in his reproach. In recovery and sobriety, we can do this. We surrender the need to be adored, praised or respected by all. We now have no need to retreat to a private place in order to indulge lust. Instead, we join Jesus outside the camp and are satisfied to be where he is. Fortunately, in a "camp" there are others who will share the burden with us, who understand both that our true reward is not here and that none of us can do this alone.

Years ago a missionary couple were returning from thirty years of overseas work. As they disembarked their ship, they noticed that the mayor of their city was being greeted by a brass band, waving streamers, balloons and a large crowd. The husband, feeling somewhat sorry for himself, remarked, "Well no at all came to welcome us." His wife paused and said, "Well dear, there is one great difference between the mayor and us. We are not home yet."

How are we to view suffering and sacrifice in the body of Christ? Protestant theology may be slightly embarrassed by the words of the Apostle Paul. "Now I rejoice in my sufferings for your sake, and in my flesh I am filling up what is lacking in Christ's afflictions for the sake of his body, that is, the church." (Colossians 1:24) Apparently, there was a connection in the great apostle's mind between Christ's sufferings and his body, the church's sufferings. He believed his own suffering was a participation in the total amount of suffering experienced by both Jesus and his followers. On the road to Damascus, after persecuting the church, Jesus said to Paul, "Why are you persecuting me?" (Acts 9:4) Was persecuting Jesus and persecuting his people the same thing? Apparently so. Each of us must bear our share. No Christian leader I know well, even the most respected and admired, has ever been free of it. Likewise, we addicts must give up control such that far from demanding pleasure on call, we can now embrace the reproach of Christ without resentment or any demand to be free of it. "Indeed, all who desire to live a godly life in Christ Jesus will be persecuted..." (2 Tim 3:12) Seeking to remove ourselves from the company of discomfort is the core of our problem. Embracing persecution, a normal sign of the Christian life, is a key sign that we have let go and are growing up in him.

Finally, the perspective of persecution is all important. "For here we have no lasting city, but we seek a city that is to come. Through him then let us continually offer up a sacrifice of praise to God, that is, the fruit of lips that acknowledge his name." (Hebrews 13:14-15) This is the perspective of eternity. We lust addicts have attempted to wrestle from this world more than it was ever capable of giving. We demanded instant medication for our bodies, souls and character defects. We failed to find lasting rest and freedom. But now, as we learn to surrender these things to Jesus, one day at a time, to invite him into our temptations and allow him to work on our character defects, an amazing reality begins to become ours. We can finally begin to let go of whatever it is that troubles us, our fears, our jealousies, our ambitions, egos, self-centeredness and resentments. This is quiet, growing and satisfying freedom that endures, not the big fix or the quixotic temporary indulgences that seduced us time and again. When we have found the God who satisfies deeply and surrendered our hearts to him, we are free.

John Donne recognized this transition and wrote about it.

"If ever any beauty I did see,

Which I desired, and got, twas but a dream of thee." (The Good-Morrow)

Seeing beauty as a window to God, rather than as an idol, sets the heart and the person free.

The City That has Foundations (Hebrews 11:10)

But there is one last freedom that awaits us. It is the freedom beyond death. The city that is to come is truly the "lasting city," There we can "drink" to our hearts content.

And he said to me, "It is done! I am the Alpha and the Omega, the beginning and the end. To the thirsty I will give from the spring of the water of life without payment. (Revelation 21: 6)

As lust addicts, we have drunk from bitter and stagnant waters most of our lives. But there, we will live beyond the reach of lust. Unlike our earthly struggle, we can quench our thirst deeply through all eternity. If we believe this is so, that it is coming and will be ours, then it is possible for us to let go in the here and now.

Since I got sober in 2010 at the age of 59, I have intermittently thought about my life from that moment until my death. I often think about the surrenders that will take place from now until my last breath. Unless I pass away suddenly, there will be the surrenders of mobility, health and friendships. Perhaps I will surrender a home or the ability to drive or travel. Then there is health and perhaps the death of my wife Claudia, unless I pre-decease her. Finally, there will be the last breath. It is said that with Rudyard Kipling's last breath, he said, "I want God." (Letting God, A. Philip Parham, Harper One, 1987, April 2nd) I may not be conscious but I would like to be. I would like to take that last breath and put it in the very bosom of God, as a gift to Him for all he has done for me. For without the one who surrendered first, who "breathed his last" and said, "Father, into your hands I commit my spirit!" (Luke 23:46), no soul and certainly no lust addict could possibly rest his breath in God. There the "fear of death" which has held people like me "in life-long bondage" will itself die.

John Donne wrote the well-known sonnet Death Be Not Proud looking forward to that moment.

Death, be not proud, though some have called thee
Mighty and dreadful, for thou art not so;
For those whom thou think'st thou dost overthrow
Die not, poor Death, nor yet canst thou kill me.
From rest and sleep, which but thy pictures be,
Much pleasure; then from thee much more must flow,
And soonest our best men with thee do go,
Rest of their bones, and soul's delivery.
Thou art slave to fate, chance, kings, and desperate men,
And dost with poison, war, and sickness dwell,
And poppy or charms can make us sleep as well
And better than thy stroke; why swell'st thou then?
One short sleep past, we wake eternally
And death shall be no more; Death, thou shalt die.

Conclusion

What God Is Up To

And the world is passing away along with its desires,
but whoever does the will of God abides forever.

(1 John 2:17)

A fad arose in high school classes a couple of decades ago. Teachers began asking students to write their own obituaries. As much as I dislike fads, I believe there is some value in this exercise. Someone once said, "Life is lived forward but understood backward." This is the best explanation for why we make mistakes when we are young. We simply do not possess the experience and perspective to make the wisest decisions. We don't understand much of what drives us until later in life and even then "only in a glass darkly." (1 Corinthians 13:12 KJV)

Jesus said to his disciples, "What I am doing you do not understand now, but afterward you will understand." (John 13:7) I have attempted to write this book from a biblical and therefore eternal perspective because the Scriptures give us the wisest and most comprehensive view of life, one not just seen from the grave backwards but from timeless eternity. One of the great ironies of life is that our deathbeds provide the best perspective on re-living life at the precise moment when there is no opportunity to do so. My goal is second-best.

It is to present a heavenly perspective in order to address an earthly problem. C.S. Lewis said, "If you read history you will find that the Christians who did most for the present world were precisely those who thought most of the next. It is since Christians have largely ceased to think of the other world that they have become so ineffective in this."(*Mere Christianity*, 1952; Harper Collins 2001, p 134.)It was once said of a saint, "Heaven was in him before he was in heaven." If something I have written smacks of a little bit of heaven for you, and you start to appropriate it now, I will be content.

My goal has been to demonstrate that the church needs now more than ever a "soul-care" view of the Scriptures which speaks to the human heart about our deepest problems, desires, and hopes. I have attempted to demonstrate that hidden within our deepest problems and struggles, like a piece of grit in an oyster, lie our greatest potential treasures. Experience has caused me to believe that one of the reasons so many addicted people, including lust addicts, are in the church today is that a deeper work is going on. God is up to something. As usual the enemy is too. He would like to discourage and demoralize us, to tell us the problem is too great to tackle or that bringing it into the light will destroy rather than help us. This is a lie. Part of this lie is a false belief that exposing our own corrupt hearts in specificity as Christians will mean that all is lost. Instead, the opposite is true. God, who raises the dead, will begin to perform untold miracles in our midst when we become honest with each other.

The Apostle Paul discovered that all his self-deceived, skin deep morality paled in comparison to the God who raises the dead, brings strength out of weakness and treats thorns in the flesh with transcendent grace. Who better to be the vehicles of hope and promise in today's church but a bunch of washed up lust addicts. If the church is to become more honest about our lust problem and devote ourselves to addressing it, the broken vessels put back together by the Potter will be of indispensible help. Many are emerging in these days as I write this. Surprisingly, many are young people in their 20's and 30's.

Part of me wishes we could gather the academic theologians and the well know Bible teachers together to get the job done. But I am afraid we are much too self-satisfied and too much in denial for that. The hour is late in the western church. No, history tells us this will be a bottom up, not a top down movement. This is the only way we can be sure God is its author and not human pride. We are in good company again.

²⁶ For consider your calling, brothers: not many of you were wise according to worldly standards,[c] not many were powerful, not many were of noble birth. ²⁷ But God chose what is foolish in the world to shame the wise; God chose what is weak in the world to shame the strong; ²⁸ God chose what is low and despised in the world, even things that are not, to bring to nothing things that are, ²⁹ so that no human being[d] might boast in the presence of God. (1 Corinthians 1:26-29)

Could history be repeating itself? The people who "turned the world upside down" were not the respectable religious led by the untainted. Their leader was accused of being a drunkard, a mere carpenter's son from a backwater town, who upset the religious money-business-as-usual in the temple and suffered an ignominious and scandalous Roman death. His followers were prostitutes, tax collectors, notorious sinners, zealots and fisherman, "unlettered men." They offered a message of hope that the lust-drenched Greco-Roman world could not ultimately resist, a message offered with love, forgiveness and inclusive welcome. Those who are surrendering lust one day at a time in the presence of Jesus are not the only rag-tag band he is using today. Not by a long shot. But he is using us to break through to a world captivated and captured by internet porn. Our goal is to help our brothers and sisters in Christ to see the challenge, bring the struggle into the open and demonstrate that lust addiction will not have the last word. We are witnesses that there is a way out that is free and beautiful and lasting, one we cannot keep to ourselves.

I used to think that God would not allow man to see him because the consequences to us would be violent and unbearable. But it may actually be otherwise. What if upon seeing God at the moment of our death, he would appear so beautiful, desirable and loving (as many who have lived through near-death experiences tell us) that we would instantaneously be filled with intense regret that we did not fully acknowledge him here, that we did not love him and serve him in the one place our free wills could make the decision to do so: here on earth. I have often thought that upon "seeing him as he is," (1 John 3:2) I would moan with the deepest of regrets. How could I not have known it was all true, every word? Why did I not give him my all? This is a remorse I am personally determined to avoid insofar as is humanly possible. What about you? It all begins when we are honest about our struggles and are willing to invite Jesus into them. He will meet us there and remarkable things will happen as we join arms together. The next step is to find others who struggle as we do. We can find them because they are living all around us, waiting for us to come out of the darkness "into his marvelous light," (1 Peter 2:9) to join our wounded hands with theirs and the one who has redeemed us all. Jesus will take us on the journey of a lifetime if we are willing to begin there.

Addendum 1

IS "LUST OR SEX ADDICT" A FALSE
LABEL FOR A CHILD OF GOD?

Over my nearly quarter of a century since first coming into sex addiction recovery, many people, including many Christian leaders have tried to talk me out of the "sex addiction" idea. They have attempted this for a variety of reasons. Many believe that lust issues are temporary and that issues of this kind go away over time. Others feel the term 'addict" is limiting, confining or a misdiagnosis. In one sense, these criticisms are accurate. For instance, many men who are experiencing a "marital crisis" will attend sex addiction recovery meetings for months and even years, but after a while, often when the marital crisis is resolved either in reconciliation or divorce, they drop out. Many stop referring to themselves as sex addicts. Furthermore, many Christian leaders will find themselves speaking to people in their congregations who are not "addicted." These people still possess some control over their behavior. Their primary ministry to these people is routine pastoral care, and Christian community bolstered by honesty and accountability. As I have indicated earlier, speaking to one's entire congregation as if we are all addicted is the way to reach everyone. Since Jesus said, "Very truly I tell you, everyone who sins is a slave to sin," (John 8:34 NIV) we are all, in a sense, addicted.

But is "sex addict" or "lust addict" really a misnomer? I believe not. If the lust issue goes away after a time or due to an external circumstance, we believe the person does not have an addiction issue. Rather, they are passing through a situational, temporary, often marital issue. Or perhaps the person was not honest with themselves about the real reason they started attending sex addiction recovery meetings. They may have been compelled to attend by a spouse, a therapist or even law enforcement. Others unfortunately believe the addiction has been eliminated, only to find out, usually after they have become attached to another person, or returned to internet porn that it has not. But if the "addiction" truly abates, the person was not an addict in the first place. Addictions are by their nature life-long. They can be "removed" but not "eliminated." Of course, many people will attempt to "control and enjoy" addictions for years and it is certainly possible for addictions to "lie in waiting" for months years or even decades before re-emerging.

The second criticism over the term "sex addiction" is that critics claim it separates us from other sinners in an unhelpful way. One Christian thought leader said recently, "we are all sexual sinners." Therefore, the argument goes, we should not identify ourselves by labels that do not appear in the Bible, especially ones that separate us from other believers. We are really all the same. But are we? In **Always Turned On** by Robert Weiss and Jennifer P. Schneider, the authors identify three distinct groups of cyber sex users, all with different behavior patterns and consequences. The authors call these The Casual Cybersex User, The At-Risk Cyber Sex User and The Addicted Cyber Sex User. Their point in using these categories is to drive home the conclusion of their research that while we may have the same vulnerabilities, we do not all possess the same sin patterns and consequences.

So as sympathetic as I am with the idea that we are all "sexual sinners," we are not all sex addicts. The person who has engaged in pre-marital sex or had an affair or looked at pornography intermittently may be a "sexual sinner," but they may simply not be a sex or lust addict. Sex addiction is progressively addictive and destructive. It involves tolerance, withdrawal and the inability to stop on one's own. It can eventuate in disease, public disgrace, imprisonment and even death. When attempting to help people diagnose themselves, we often will use the Twenty Questions. Here they are.

1. Have you ever thought you needed help for your sexual thinking or behavior?
2. That you'd be better off if you didn't keep "giving in"?
3. That sex or stimuli are controlling you?
4. Have you ever tried to stop or limit doing what you felt was wrong in your sexual behavior?
5. Do you resort to sex to escape, relieve anxiety, or because you can't cope?
6. Do you feel guilt, remorse, or depression afterward?
7. Has your pursuit of sex become more compulsive?
8. Does it interfere with relations with your spouse?
9. Do you have to resort to images or memories during sex?
10. Does an irresistible impulse arise when the other party makes the overtures or sex is offered?
11. Do you keep going from one relationship or lover to another?
12. Do you feel the right relationship would help you stop lusting, masturbating, or being so promiscuous
13. Do you have a destructive need—a desperate sexual or emotional need for someone?
14. Does pursuit of sex make you careless for yourself or the welfare of your family or others?
15. Has your effectiveness or concentration decreased as sex has become more compulsive?
16. Do you lose time from work for it?
17. Do you turn to a lower environment when pursuing sex?
18. Do you want to get away from the sex partner as soon as possible after the act?
19. Although your spouse is sexually compatible, do you still masturbate or have sex with others?
20. Have you ever been arrested for a sex related offense?

Jay Haug

Answers to these questions will vary greatly. However, those troubled by their own sexual behavior may find answering them helpful to understanding whether sexaholism is a core problem for them or not.

Finally, critics of sex addiction call it a false label because they say it hangs an ill-defined horse collar around a person's neck that creates a burden rather than an opportunity for growth. There is some truth in this. Certainly, it is possible for people to hide behind the "sex addiction" label. Many have used it to excuse or justify their behavior or their inability to stop. But far more people, particularly those who have embraced long-term sobriety have found the idea of accepting their own sex addiction to be liberating. Why?

In my own case, I was able to find liberty by finally accepting what was truly wrong with me. All the unanswered questions about why I behaved as I did and why I could not stop despite my Christian faith were answered by the sex addiction recovery program. They were not answered by church teaching or theology, unfortunately. At least not immediately. However, when I was able to accept who I truly was and what was truly wrong with me and embrace a recovery program, what happened? I came back to church and the Scriptures and found truth bursting out of its pages. I understood 'the thorn in the flesh" (2 Corinthians 12) for the first time. I understood that God wanted me to help others who struggled.

Certain passages became a life line to me. Here is one "3 Blessed be the God and Father of our Lord Jesus Christ, the Father of mercies and God of all comfort, 4 who comforts us in all our affliction, so that we may be able to comfort those who are in any affliction, with the comfort with which we ourselves are comforted by God. (2 Corinthians 1:3) Most importantly, I began to walk with Jesus more closely in a more immediate sense, be more open with people, especially my wife, and serve others. Yes, I am a sexual sinner among others in the church, but I also understand my own sexual brokenness for the first time and I could not have come to the place of peace and usefulness I inhabit today without this particular understanding of sex addiction and the specific growth plan laid out to overcome it.

Addendum 2

HEALING PRAYER, LUST AND SEXUAL ADDICTION

Many will wonder where the role of healing prayer fits in relieving lust and sexual addiction. We believe that prayer is essential, especially as it expresses the deep connection with Jesus as our lust- bearer. We have faith in an "all of the above approach," when it comes to healing prayer and all aspects of recovery. This has worked for us and includes morning devotions, evening prayer including an evaluation of the day's lust and character defect occurrences and prayer for protection in dreams throughout the night. As recovery continues lustful dreams should subside in sobriety, especially if we pray that they will, aligning our will with God's. Immediate, in the heat of the moment prayers of surrender throughout the day are essential as we face difficulties and challenges. As we employ these prayers habitually, they become easier to engage in over time. "Lord, please help that person to find what they are looking for. Jesus, thank you for being my lust bearer. Please take this away right now. I don't want it and I surrender it to you and thank you for bearing it for me." Surrender is our "get out of jail free card" and the more we employ it the more our connection with Jesus is solidified. This does not obviate the need to make a phone call to a fellow struggler whom we may need to bring into our struggle. We cannot do this alone. Recovery is a multifaceted experience in which all the building blocks are essential, prayer being number one.

What about healing prayer? No question this can be helpful. Some people in recovery have used a healing technique which brings Jesus into early childhood experiences in order to replace foundational lies which have led to addictive behavior. (My two foundational lies were "I am all alone and there is no one who will help me" and "Sex is my most important need." My replacement truths are: I am not alone and was not alone. Jesus was with me every step of the way and continues to be. I believe his promises that he will be "until the end of the age." (Matthew 28:20) Sex is not my most important need because I now have healthier ways to deal with character defects, like fear, resentment and isolation, freeing me to experience sexuality in the way God intended it.) Many people in recovery testify that reintegrating their traumatizing experience in the presence of Jesus has brought the "split-off" part of themselves back, leading to a deeper healing and acceptance of their personal histories.

No prayer is ever wasted and we should construct lives that "pray without ceasing." (1 Thessalonians 5:17) In addition to redirecting lust and surrendering character defects in prayer as we draw near to the Lord, we can find a deeper rest and spiritual freedom as we dwell in his presence.

Why do some people say that prayer did not deliver them from their addiction, even diligent prayer exercised over decades? Ultimately, we may not know why this is so. We experience many prayers we call "unanswered" in many areas of our lives. We struggle to accept prayers that seem to get "no" or "not yet" as an answer.

But the reason deliverance from addiction does not respond to prayer may be tied up in the "mystery of lawlessness." (2 Thessalonians 2:7). Why did Adam and Eve who were created without sin nevertheless choose it? Even when we ask to be prayed for and submit to prayer, our will can remain captive to our addictive disease. We may be unconsciously holding on to it, while at the same time wanting God to instantaneously remove it like a cancerous tumor. Double-mindedness can stunt our spiritual growth. (James 1:8)

But addiction often seems not to yield to the quick fix. We can be like a child with a band aid on a cut who says to his parent, "Just rip it off," in order to resolve the pain in a moment. There is no doubt this kind of healing sometimes happens. But in my experience it is infrequent. There is a deeper wound that needs attention. We would like to be rid of our problem, but sometimes a deeper work is going on that cannot be hurried. I personally had to experience a 17 year bottom before I surrendered.

How can we understand such a long time for healing to take place? God is greater than our hearts and his timing is perfect. He has given us the gift of free will and seems to be unwilling to take it back, even in the case of those who want nothing to do with him, either in this world or the next. Surrender is ours to give or withhold.

Pope John Paul II puts it this way. "Nobody can use a person as a means toward an end, not yet God the Creator. On the part of God, indeed, it is totally out of the question, since, by giving man an intelligent and free nature, he has thereby ordained that each man alone will decide for himself the ends of his activity, and not be a blind tool of someone else's ends. Therefore, if God intends to direct man toward certain goals, he allows him to begin with to know those goals, so that he may make them his own and strive toward them independently. In this amongst other things resides the most profound logic of revelation: God allows man to learn his supernatural ends, but the decision to strive toward an end, the choice of course, is left to man's free will. God does not redeem man against his will." (Theology of the Body Explained, p.490)

What we have experienced in sexual addiction ministry is that many people after years of struggling and sometimes being bathed in the prayers of others, finally surrender to God and the program of recovery. What we discover in examining the personal histories of these people is that God has been working in their lives and arranging circumstances, including their own personal suffering, to bring about this change. So, as we pray for ourselves and others, we should remember that God brings about transformation in his time, not ours. In the meantime, we should continue to pray, to seek, to ask and knock for those suffering with lust, pornography and sexual addiction. A key sign that we have not given up hope for those who struggle is that we continue to pray to the God who hears and answers. There can be no deeper healing than the one shown forth in the one bound for many years who receives the grace to let go. Like the woman "who had been subject to bleeding for twelve years. [26] She had suffered a great deal under the care of many doctors and had spent all she had, yet instead of getting better she grew worse." (Mark 5: 25b-26). The story of our getting worse before we get better is all part of the sovereign story of a loving God whose plans are his to execute. We will have to look to eternity to explain the things now hidden from our eyes.

Notes

1. A brief excerpt from the Big Book, *Alcoholics Anonymous* is reprinted with permission of Alcoholics Anonymous World Services, Inc. ("A.A.W.S.") Permission to reprint an excerpt does not mean that A.A.W.S. has reviewed or approved the contents of this publication, or that A.A.W.S. necessarily agrees with the views expressed herein. A.A. is a program of recovery from alcoholism only – use of these excerpts in connection with programs and activities which are patterned after A.A., but which address other problems, or in any other non A.A. context, does not imply otherwise. A.A. is a spiritual program, A.A. is not a religious program. Thus, AA is not affiliated or allied with any sect, denomination or religious belief and nothing in this publication implies otherwise."

2. The 12 Steps of Sexaholics Anonymous

1. We admitted that we were powerless over lust -- that our lives had become unmanageable.
2. Came to believe that a Power greater than ourselves could restore us to sanity.

3. Made a decision to turn our will and our lives over to the care of God as we understood Him.

4. Made a searching and fearless moral inventory of ourselves.

5. Admitted to God, to ourselves, and to another human being the exact nature of our wrongs.

6. Were entirely ready to have God remove all these defects of character.

7. Humbly asked Him to remove our shortcomings.

8. Made a list of all persons we had harmed, and became willing to make amends to them all.

9. Made direct amends to such people wherever possible, except when to do so would injure them or others.

10. Continued to take personal inventory and when we were wrong, promptly admitted it.

11. Sought through prayer and meditation to improve our conscious contact with God as we understood Him, praying only for knowledge of His will for us and the power to carry that out.

12. Having had a spiritual awakening as the result of these Steps, we tried to carry this message to sexaholics, and to practice these principles in all our affairs.

Bibliography and Recommended Reading

Ron. J., Impossible Joy, Liberia, Simi Valley (Available from Royk.com), 2011.

Ron J., Lust Virus, Liberia, Simi Valley (Available from Royk.com)

Christopher West, Theology of the Body Explained, A Commentary of John Paul II's Man and Woman He Created Them, 2007.

Robert Weiss and Jennifer P. Schneider, Always Turned On, Sex Addiction in the Digital Age. Gentle Path Press, 2015

John Eldredge, The Journey of Desire, Thomas Nelson, 2000.

Michael John Cusick, Surfing for God, Discovering the Divine Desire Beneath Sexual Struggle, Thomas Nelson, 2012.

Sharon Hersh, The Last Addiction, Why Self-Help is Not Enough, Waterbrook Press, 2008.

Dr. Bob and the Good Old Timers, AA World Services, 1980.

Dallas Willard, The Divine Conspiracy, Fount, 2008.

John Piper, Desiring God, John Piper Paperback, 2011.

Jonathan Daugherty, Secrets, A True Story of Addiction, Infidelity and Second Chances, Tate Publishing, 2009.

Richard Rohr, Breathing Under Water, Franciscan Media, 2011.

Rosaria Champagne Butterfield, The Secret Thoughts of An Unlikely Convert, Crown and Covenant Publications, 2012

A. Philip Parham, Letting God, Christian Meditations for Recovery, Harper One, New York, 1987.

Nate Larkin, Samson and the Pirate Monks, Thomas Nelson, 2006.

Jay Haug, Speaking to the Addictive Personality in the Local Congregation, Create Space, 2014

Jay Haug, Beyond the Flaming Sword, Create Space, 2012.